This book attacks the assumption found in much moral philosophy that social control, as such, is an intellectually and morally destructive force. It replaces this view with a richer and deeper perspective on the nature of social character, aimed at showing how social freedom cannot mean immunity from social pressure.

The author demonstrates how our competence as rational and social agents depends on a constructive adaption of social control mechanisms. Our facility at achieving our goals is enhanced, rather than undermined, by social control. The author then articulates sources and degrees of legitimate social control in different social and historical settings.

Drawing on a wide range of literature in moral and political philosophy, law, cognitive and social psychology, and anthropology (not to mention some very perceptive readings of novels by Henry James), Professor Schoeman shows how the aim of moral philosophy ought to be to understand our social character, not to establish fortifications against it in the name of rationality and autonomy.

Privacy and social freedom

Cambridge Studies in Philosophy and Public Policy

GENERAL EDITOR: Douglas MacLean

The purpose of this series is to publish the most innovative and up-to-date research into the values and concepts that underlie major aspects of public policy. Hitherto most research in this field has been empirical. This series is primarily conceptual and normative; that is, it investigates the structure of arguments and the nature of values relevant to the formation, justification, and criticism of public policy. At the same time it is informed by empirical considerations, addressing specific issues, general policy concerns, and the methods of policy analysis and their applications.

The books in the series are inherently interdisciplinary and include anthologies as well as monographs. They are of particular interest to philosophers, political and social scientists, economists, policy analysts, and those involved in public administration and environmental policy.

Privacy and social freedom

FERDINAND DAVID SCHOEMAN

UNIVERSITY OF SOUTH CAROLINA

CAMBRIDGE
UNIVERSITY PRESS

Published by the Press Syndicate of the University of Cambridge
The Pitt Building, Trumpington Street, Cambridge CB2 1RP
40 West 20th Street, New York, NY 10011–4211, USA
10 Stamford Road, Oakleigh, Victoria 3166, Australia

© Cambridge University Press 1992

First published in 1992

Printed in the United States of America

Library of Congress Cataloging-in-Publication Data
Schoeman, Ferdinand David.
Privacy and social freedom / Ferdinand David Schoeman.
p.   cm. – (Cambridge studies in philosophy and public policy)
Includes bibliographical references and index.
ISBN 0-521-41564-0
1. Privacy, Right of.   2. Privacy.   I. Title.   II. Series.
JC596.S36   1992
323.44′8 – dc20   91–40062
CIP

A catalog record for this book is available from the British Library

ISBN 0-521-41564-0 hardback

For Sara Ann Schechter-Schoeman

Contents

Acknowledgments

My first extended opportunity to focus on privacy was afforded me in 1982 by Jerry Skolnick with an invitation to
teach a course on privacy in the Jurisprudence and Social
Policy Program at the University of California at Berkeley.
This was a wonderful occasion for me, one that still rever-
berates in so many ways. I am indebted to the faculty of that
program for providing such an enriching environment.

I was fortunate enough to receive a Rockefeller Foundation
fellowship to work on my privacy project. Under the terms
of this fellowship, I spent an academic year (1984–5) at the
Institute for Philosophy and Public Policy at the University
of Maryland. Not only did the fellowship free me completely
from any responsibilities that might compete with research,
but the academic and personal support provided by the permanent staff and another visiting fellow (Amy Guttman) of
that institute was ideal. My associations with people who
were at the institute continue to provide support for me, for
which I am very grateful. At a time when, because of serious
illness, it was unclear whether I would be able to guide this
book through necessary and helpful revisions, Claudia Mills
offered to work with readers' comments in revising the text.
Douglas MacLean, editor of the series in which this book
appears, provided me with both the encouragement and in-
cisive criticisms that helped make the book better than it
otherwise would have been.

When I was in Maryland, Stanley Benn was visiting at
Johns Hopkins University. Stanley, a profound and creative

researcher in the philosophy of privacy, and a treasure to the discipline as a whole, was kind enough to schedule a number of conversations with me about privacy in general and about my own work in particular. These conversations are recalled with utmost appreciation.

During the academic year 1988–9, funding by the National Endowment for the Humanities permitted me to continue my work on privacy. The fall semester of that year was again spent at Boalt Hall in Berkeley, this time as a visiting scholar under arrangements with the Earl Warren Institute. I am most grateful to Franklin Zimring, director of the Institute, for the opportunity and support offered me. The Center for Law and Society, under the direction of Malcolm Feeley, provided me with two opportunities to elaborate my work in front of a distinguished audience. These opportunities helped me organize my efforts and focus my attention in productive ways. Of particular value to me during my time at Berkeley was making the acquaintance of Robert Post, a fellow traveler in the area of privacy. Robert showered me with the most stimulating and enriching insights into the cultural and philosophical dimensions of privacy. Since then he has afforded me timely, constructive, honest, and inspired comments on a version of this book, for which I am most grateful. While I was at Berkeley, several conversations I had with Bernard Williams and Richard Wollheim helped me advance my project.

During the spring of 1989, the University of South Carolina Law School appointed me a visiting scholar while I was still an NEH fellow. I was provided with all the accommodations a researcher could wish, including opportunities to try out ideas at faculty colloquiums.

The Frances Lewis Law Center at the Washington and Lee Law School appointed me scholar-in-residence for the spring term of 1990. Again I was provided with ideal conditions for pursuing my research. I used this opportunity to organize and fashion this research into a book. Research assistants at the center – Lee Hays Romano, Anne Compson, and Beth Nightingale — deserve acknowledgment for helping me organize my thoughts into tolerable English and for providing me with incentives for having something for them to read every week. Lee Romano, in particular, distinguished herself in dedicating hour after hour to reading and rereading chapters and in suggesting constructions that would help make my thoughts intelligible.

In addition to Robert Post and Douglas MacLean, Michael Slote, Richard Burgh, and Ruth Gavison provided me with detailed comments on the entire manuscript. The help they afforded me is most deeply and sincerely appreciated.

Even greater than my debt to these scholars and institutions is my debt to Sara Schechter-Schoeman. My own extended excursions were graced with the excitement of being free to do my own work in wonderfully stimulating places. The person who lost out because of these indulgences was my wife. This cannot be compensated. Nor can her expressions of confidence and trust be repaid, however much appreciated and treasured.

Before my book was accepted for publication, I was diagnosed as having leukemia. For being able to reach this day, I am indebted to many people: first to my physicians – James McFarland of Columbia, South Carolina, and Jean Henslee, Edward Romond, Jan Gyarfas, and Edward Harder of Lexington, Kentucky – for life-sustaining treatments; next to the staff who cared for me at Richland Memorial Hospital, Columbia, South Carolina; then to Dr. Thomas McCullough of Columbia, South Carolina, for teaching me that I can be more than a victim of such a disease; then to family and friends from near and far who demonstrated to me that the life I was fighting to sustain was a life worth struggling for; and finally, to my three "guardian angels": Miriam Schoeman, my daughter, whose bone marrow gives me a new chance at life; Dmitri Schoeman, my son, who encouraged me with his confidence, and diverted me with chess; and Sara Schechter-Schoeman, whose support, love, strength, and determination were, and continue to be, manifested in too many ways to detail.

Introduction

This book evolved from my effort to relate three areas of personal and professional interest: privacy, social freedom, and human social nature. First is privacy. When I began writing about privacy – at the time, I thought of it as writing about intimacy – I was convinced that there are central domains of human social and moral life that are ill-suited to being characterized by any of the standard competing moral and legal theories.[1] In an early essay, I argued that properly understanding the moral dimensions of parent–child relationships requires us to recognize the limits of both utilitarian and rights-centered autonomy-promoting approaches. I still believe this.

My concern with privacy in this book is not focused primarily on the claims of privacy that can be made against governments. Rather, I aim to understand the dimensions of privacy that arise in our social encounters. I argue that privacy in the contexts of our social relations protects us from social overreaching – limits the control of others over our lives. Understanding how privacy works in the social context is more complicated than understanding how privacy works in the governmental context. One reason for this difference is that immunity from certain forms of social control typically is not a blanket prohibition directed against all others but is selectively directed. Appreciating this difference will provide some insight into the debate over whether so-called life-choice issues – issues of birth control, including abortion;

sexual orientation; use of recreational drugs; and so forth –
are properly categorized as autonomy or privacy issues.

In addition to offering an analysis of privacy in the social
context, I offer some historical and speculative material that
situates privacy in a social process. I believe that we better
understand concepts when we see their historical roles and
their web of relationships in diverse settings. Rather than
leading to relativism, this approach deepens our grasp of the
importance of privacy in our own context.

A second interest pursued in this book is social freedom.
Although the political and legal approaches to privacy have
been illuminating and important, they have omitted an especially important dimension of privacy: the form and function of privacy in promoting *social* freedom. Clearly, we are
all concerned with the encroachment of the state into people's private lives; but, equally clearly, we are ever mindful
of this threat. With varying degrees of success, we continually interpret our constitutions and design our laws to protect people from governmental overreaching. We expend
much effort in defining the contours of overreaching and in
framing institutional defenses and remedies.

Yet this other domain, the social domain in which privacy
plays a critical role, remains philosophically unexplored despite being central to our everyday experiences. We cannot
take for granted that the sorts of strategies and analyses that
are appropriate in the political domain are also appropriate
in the social domain. The presupposition that the domains
are the same or close enough to be treated as if they were
the same represents the extent to which privacy in the social
context is conceived in the literature. John Stuart Mill wrote
his great essay *On Liberty* to change public consciousness in
ways that would better protect people from *social* overreaching. He was concerned that we are *more* vulnerable to the
insidious control of other citizens than we are to the tyran-
nical impulses of government. Yet present-day uses of the
essay focus on the relatively brief discussion Mill devotes to
governments and leave unexplored what Mill took to be most
important. To my knowledge, there is no recent evaluation

of Mill's approach to the primary problem he addresses – protecting people from *social* overreaching – that does not simply assume that protecting people from social overreaching is the same problem and requires the same solutions as protecting people from governmental overreaching. I aim to correct this by focusing interest on conditions for social freedom.

In the process of focusing on social freedom, I suggest that our usual approach toward human susceptibility to social influence is completely misguided and unrealistic. Philosophers are fond of telling us that people are free, or act autonomously, only to the extent that they judge and act on reasons that are issue-relevant. Reasons are issue-relevant when they exclude doing or believing things because that is what others expect of one, except in special cases that involve conventions and coordination. More conditions are required for freedom, but this one of social independence is necessary. It follows that when we act because of social pressures, or because we want to conform to what we see around us, we are less than free, less than rational, less than autonomous. This outlook is misguided both about what it is reasonable to expect of individuals and about the conditions of social freedom. Much of what is most important about our life would be lost, would be inaccessible to us, were we uninfluenced – unpressured, if you will – by what we see around us. Most, if not all, of our effectiveness as social agents would be undermined by the elimination of the kinds of pressures and influences that philosophers in the analytic tradition treat as rationally corrupting. My reasoning for this claim can be summarized as follows: Most of our protections from a monolithic social and political tyranny depend on participation in associations. The survival and effectiveness of these associations presuppose the availability of forces to bring about conformity with group norms – forces such as loyalty to group participants, methods, and ends. Yet these very forces that are central to group life and social effectiveness are deemed unbefitting in several of the analytic philosophical circles.

This brings me to my third interest: human nature. People do not function generally in the way philosophers, especially those concerned with ethics and social and legal philosophy, suggest or presuppose. One representation of people the most distinguished and inspired writing portrays is that of cognitively and morally autonomous beings who are able to sort out issues for themselves and are responsible for doing so. This autonomy is expressed in the principle that one should judge and act only on the basis of reasons that a fully reasonable and rational person would consider relevant. The reference to reasons a fully reasonable and rational person would consider reflects the position that morality is a type of rationality, a rationality that can be explicated without reference to a particular culture.[2] The influence of others or of culture generally, except when this influence presents arguments for rational evaluation, is not just worrisome but generally is considered inappropriate. Standard treatments suggest that people should not be susceptible to nonrational appeals by others.

Observed patterns of failure to live up to this standard of rationality are not thought to impugn the legitimacy of the expectation that people behave rationally. The expectation is regarded as an ideal; and, it is stressed, patterns of failings do not undermine ideals. Ironically, many philosophers regard economic or decision-theoretic models of rationality as misguided for the kinds of reasons that they treat as irrelevant in evaluating the adequacy of these moral ideals. Let me explain. Models of economic rationality – models that are extended to all decision areas through the device of utilities – purport to be both roughly descriptive and precisely normative. Why should a proponent of this model, particularly one who stresses the normative dimension of the model, feel threatened by being shown that people characteristically judge differently from the way that the theory prescribes? The answer is that these models omit too much of what is humanly important. These omissions disqualify the theories, both normatively and descriptively. They cannot be trusted as intuition-displacing algorithms of action. The disparity between ordinary thought and the outcomes prescribed by the models is seen to reflect badly on the models. I believe the same is true of moral theory.[3] Standard presuppositions about human aims and competences are so misguided as to be relegated to the same questionable status as the economic models just discussed.[4]

My criticism of the typical models of human nature is that they are oblivious of our existence as cultural beings and discordant with empirical discoveries in social and cognitive psychology. Seeking remedies for the blindness and discordance just cited requires efforts to coordinate empirical and interpretive responses. Recently, there has been a convergence in cognitive discoveries and theories that suggests that any plausible model of the brain would have to employ various strategies or heuristics, fallible shortcuts, to accomplish its multifarious tasks. From cues about how we work, we gain insight about what we are like, what we seek, and what we can do to achieve our goals. In turn, this insight portrays some things about the structure and limitations of human nature that moral theories ignore to their peril.

An aspect of the structure and limits of human nature that tends to be ignored by moral theory is that we cannot adequately understand human moral nature by disregarding our cultural dependencies and our social vulnerabilities. I construe moral philosophy as aimed at understanding our social character rather than as establishing fortifications against it in the name of rationality and autonomy.

A major tradition of moral theory generally sees cultural susceptibilities and socializing tendencies as standing in the way of moral understanding, moral abilities, and moral fulfillment in autonomous living. I propose an understanding of moral philosophy that seeks to integrate, rather than exclude, our experience as socially dependent beings. An important aspect of this understanding is showing that being culturally embedded is not the same as ritually and unreflectively mimicking whatever others do. Cultural embeddedness allows more subtlety than this equation suggests. We have no reason whatsoever to think that those who are culturally sensitive are more disposed to morally outrageous conduct than those who are oblivious of cultural norms. Indeed, we have every reason to think otherwise.

Establishing an alternative focus for moral philosophy will promote appreciation of the importance of privacy as a social category. The following steps help explain this connection between the redirection of moral theory and an improved understanding of privacy. Because of the sort of cognitive and emotional system we are, we cannot be the rational and autonomous beings envisioned in so much philosophical posturing. In fact, it is our dependence on others – our cognitive, emotional, cultural, and material dependence – that accounts for most of our moral qualities. (It can do this and, at the same time, account for most of our vices.) Our dependence on others also accounts for most of what we are and can hope to become. First we must see this dependence as at least partly a strength. Our disposition to adopt rules and roles by which we share life may provide the basis for morality in a way far different from that suggested by the dominant moral theories – contractarian or consequentialist. Being susceptible to what others think and to how they act is a feature not to be extinguished but to be nurtured in a controlled way.

Our susceptibility to others is a prime and salutary feature of being human. But it also threatens us, which is why privacy comes back into play. In different historical settings, and in different contexts within one historical setting, different levels of susceptibility to others are appropriate. The practice of privacy, not as a right but as a system of nuanced social norms, modulates the effectiveness of social control over an individual. Recognition of the constructive role of social influence and social pressure forces us to concede that people are influenced appropriately by factors beyond those generally sanctioned in moral theory and philosophy. We cannot substitute for the sorts of judgment of which we are capable the sort of rational judgment advocated in liberal theories and remain socially, morally, practically, and intellectually competent beings. It is good, in sum, that we are subject to forces and pressures we do not monitor and judge. It is good that we are driven to be like others and care what they think about how we behave and about what we are like. It is good that we accept much that we cannot defend, if challenged, and to that extent act heteronomously.

In various settings, different levels of self-direction are appropriate. We use standards of social privacy both to acknowledge the point and to modulate the influence of informal means of social control.

Privacy protects social freedom by limiting scrutiny by others and the control some of them have over our lives. Yet we must search for an interpretation of social freedom that is consistent with what we know about human cognitive and motivational tendencies and illuminates the fundamental role freedom plays. Furthermore, and critically, our interpretation of social freedom should be cognizant of the opportunities for effective social agency social groups exclusively afford individual participants. Social freedom cannot mean immunity from social influence and pressure. Rather, social freedom is available to the extent that there are options among associative ties, each of which appropriately exploits social forces to maintain coherence and effectiveness for social action. In this respect, social freedom is quite different from political freedom. In some contexts it is appropriate for people to use social control mechanisms to achieve ends where both the ends and means would be illegitimate for the liberal state.

Human nature being what it is, privacy is indispensable in a community that recognizes social freedom as a good, but a restructuring of our philosophical picture of social dynamics is needed to see why this is so. Normative aspects of this restructuring occasion a different representation of the role of moral philosophy.

Admittedly, the association of themes here seems peculiar. In the course of this book, the connections should become clearer. Chapter 1 addresses the meaning and scope of privacy. In that context, I indicate two discrete usages or roles of our notion of privacy that are not differentiated in the burgeoning literature. I also describe the relations between privacy, emotional vulnerability, and morality. This background enables me to resolve the controversy over whether "personal choice" issues such as abortion and birth control are properly characterized as privacy issues. It also enables me to argue that privacy is important largely because of how it facilitates association with people, not independence from people. This approach suggests that the identification of the right to privacy with the right to be left alone is an incomplete and misleading characterization. These latter themes are further developed in Chapter 8. In Chapter 2, I discuss John Stuart Mill's advocacy of individuality and his account of how various social responses either fostered or frustrated the emergence of individuality. Mill so radically mismeasured humanity that the strategy he thought would lead to our liberation from stifling social forces amplifies our exposure and vulnerability to these forces. He replaced privacy with a confidence in rational independence. In this he erred. His error is instructive because it is shared by so many eminent writers today.

In Chapter 3, I introduce some major contemporary figures in moral, social, and legal philosophy and show that Mill's legacy extends to them as well. Like Mill's their confidence in the independence of human judgment obscures central features of moral life. I demonstrate that it is common among philosophers to equate being culturally influenced and being philosophically or morally corrupted. In Chapter 4, I introduce some findings from social psychology to draw a picture of human nature and social judgment that is quite different from that commonly represented in philosophical literature. I show that the standards for properly vindicated rational and moral thought advocated by Mill and his philosophical heirs seem to ignore what we know about human judgment from other sources.

In Chapter 5, I recommend a different orientation for moral and social philosophy, one that is more attuned to our social and cognitive nature than the dominant theories are. I argue here that appropriately we *are* subject to the judgment and pressure of others. Moreover, an understanding of social life that missed this would be missing perhaps the central feature of moral life – the prospect of a culturally enriched, civilized life with others.

In Chapter 6, I advance a social theory that explains why privacy is important and how it functions to protect people in ordinary social contexts, while leaving them open to appropriate levels of social influence and pressure. Here I show how privacy is critical to the aims of social life articulated in the preceding chapter. There emerges a theory of social freedom, which I view not as freedom from social influence as such but as freedom from overreaching social control. People are socially free to the extent that two conditions are met: Their culture provides them with alternative, function-specific associative prospects; and the sorts of social control mechanisms used on these people within their associations are fitting, given the ends of the association.

In Chapter 7, I present a cultural history of privacy to illustrate the point of the distinction in ordinary uses of privacy, and I introduce empirical data for more theoretical claims I make in subsequent chapters.

Using themes developed earlier in the book, I address in Chapter 8 what seems to be a contradiction between the function of the social practice of privacy, on the one hand, and the function of the social practice of gossip, on the other. Whereas privacy seems to restrict access to people, gossip exposes people. I use the discussion of the relationship between privacy and gossip to illustrate how privacy does not function by acting in opposition to social norms but is integrated and interdependent with other social practices. Acknowledging this helps us appreciate how privacy is beneficial for socialization, not something that sets individuals off against others.

In Chapter 9, I introduce the notion of 'spheres of life', relate this to the previous discussion of associative ties, and clarify the connection of spheres of life with moral and social judgment, especially as this judgment concerns privacy. I argue that spheres of life have implicit privacy norms built in, whether these spheres relate to what we consider public or private dimensions of a person's life. It follows that privacy norms relate to public roles as they do to private roles.

Having discussed how privacy norms function in public life to modulate social freedom, I turn in Chapter 10 to discuss how privacy structures private life. Specifically, I examine how morality in private spheres functions differently from morality in public spheres. What emerges from this discussion is the extent to which the contours of morality portrayed as representative in moral theory belong to the branch of morality that regulates public spheres. Because most of our active moral dealings arise in the private domain, the identification of morality with public-sphere morality reflects a misguided emphasis, as well as a biased supply of paradigms for moral thinking generally. Except for a brief epilogue, this discussion ends my elaboration of how reflection on privacy forces us to reexamine human nature and some fundamental tenets of contemporary moral theory.

Some years ago, I attended a series of lectures by Saul Kripke on identity. At one point during this series, he took a rubber band and snapped it. He did this to illustrate simply that the standard philosophical picture of identity of a physical object that requires spatial and temporal contiguity is not inevitably part of our everyday experience. We have no trouble thinking of the rubber band as being one and the same before and after the snap, even though we lose track of its course and stages in between. Wherever it is in between, whether these stages are contiguous or not, and this is something we cannot really tell, these stages are consistent with our principles of identity.

Similarly, much of what I have to say about the philosophical theories I discuss is unassuming and involves points that anyone who is not committed to promoting a theory would find commonplace. There are some simple truths that I believe philosophers have missed. I do little more than point to some of these truths and discuss some of their implications. Dramatic changes in perspective are required to make philosophy reflect these truths accurately.

Chapter 1

The meaning and scope of privacy

After reviewing some contexts in which privacy predominates as an issue, I shall show that there are two very different kinds of privacy, serving diametrically opposed functions vis-à-vis social control over the individual. I shall discuss the difference between these sorts of privacy and point out the significance of, and basis for, seeing one form of privacy as protecting people from the overreaching control of others.

ON NOT DEFINING PRIVACY

Often it is suggested that the best way to begin a discussion of a volatile and controversial concept like privacy is with a definition. However, given the socially hyperactive role that privacy plays in contemporary controversies regarding the evolving contours of personhood, there may be some benefit in not striving for verbal precision in defining privacy before this evolution is further played out. At this stage, we can better understand privacy by characterizing the contexts in which it arises or is invoked as a concern. The particular contexts considered here, beginning with the legal context, were chosen because they are germane to the issues that arise in this book and not because they are representative of all privacy contexts or controversies, let alone comprehensive. We shall see from the discussion that nearly everything about privacy, from its scope to its value, is controversial.

THE LEGAL CONTEXT: A SKETCH

Privacy has been described in a U.S. Supreme Court decision as a right more fundamental than any of the rights enumerated in the Bill of Rights. However, privacy attracted scant explicit legal attention until 1890, when Warren and Brandeis advocated explicit legal recognition of a right to privacy.[1] The fourth amendment to the U.S. Constitution guarantees the right to be secure in one's person, houses, papers, and effects against unreasonable search or seizure. The first amendment affords people free exercise of religion and freedom of speech, the press, and assembly – freedoms we associate with freedom of conscience. In *Stanley v. Georgia*,[2] this amendment was cited as limiting the government's competence to control the contents of thoughts. The fifth amendment ensures that people cannot be required to testify against themselves, and the fourteenth amendment provides that they cannot be deprived of life, liberty, or property without due process of law.

Two other areas of law have also evolved in a way that is protective of privacy. In tort law, there are four categories of individual protection: (1) intrusion upon a person's seclusion, solitude, or private affairs; (2) public disclosure of private, embarrassing facts; (3) public disclosure of a person in a false light; (4) appropriation of another's name, image, or other aspect of identity, for one's advantage or profit, without that person's consent.

The most controversial treatment of privacy in the law arises in the recent Supreme Court decisions that recognize "procreative rights" like the relatively unencumbered rights to choose a marriage partner (*Loving v. Virginia*),[3] to use birth control (*Griswold v. Connecticut, Eisenstadt v. Baird, Carey v. Population Services International*),[4] to become a parent (*Skinner v. Oklahoma*),[5] to have access to abortion services (*Roe v. Wade*),[6] and, at least in the setting of a marriage, the right to engage in unregulated sexual practices (*Bowers v. Hardwick*).[7] Among those who recognize these rights as bona fide privacy rights, controversy exists concerning whether they are attached primarily to people when part of an actual or potential marriage situation or whether they apply to individuals in intimate contexts irrespective of the potential for marriage (*Bowers v. Hardwick*). (There are contexts in which privacy-related privileges that are accorded spouses are revoked when third parties, including the couple's children, are present.)

Much controversy exists concerning whether these procreative rights have constitutional bases and whether they actually turn on concern for privacy. Many would argue that these are strictly issues of autonomy, concerning as they do the locus of control over choices in living, and only tangentially raise issues of privacy, a concept pertaining exclusively to informational or physical access to a person. But this representation of the issue is misleading.

The debate about the constitutional basis for privacy helps illustrate that there are broader and narrower conceptions of privacy. On the narrow end of the spectrum, privacy relates exclusively to personal information and describes the extent to which others have access to this information. There is an even narrower conception, one that limits the range of privacy to personal information that is "undocumented."[8] A broader conception extends beyond the informational domain and encompasses anonymity and restricted physical access. The most embracing characterizations of privacy include aspects of autonomy, particularly those associated with control over the intimacies of personal identity. For advocates of this interpretation, privacy is the measure of the extent an individual is afforded the social and legal space to develop the emotional, cognitive, spiritual, and moral powers of an autonomous agent.[9] An advocate of one of the narrower conceptions can agree about the value of autonomous development but think that privacy, as properly defined, makes an important, yet limited contribution to its achievement.

SOME FEMINISTS' PERSPECTIVES

Another area of debate within the privacy literature is whether the public–private distinction functions primarily as a social control mechanism to maintain the dominance of groups in power and to enforce silence and helplessness on others. The institutions of privacy are seen as instruments for the marginalization of those without power. Within the private realm, the differences between male and female perspectives are lost, not in the shared intimacy of our professed aspirations but in rejection of the female perspective altogether. The subordination of women to the male outlook evident in the public world is mirrored and allowed to run its course in the private world, "inaccessible to, unaccountable to . . . anything beyond itself."[10] Our institution of privacy keeps women domesticated, isolated, and thus politically and ideologically voiceless.

The private dimensions have been associated with the domestic, personal, intimate, familial, female- or child-related, or small-group or intimate contexts. The argument continues that relegating these realms to the normatively private sustains unfair power relationships and fails to recognize the responsibility to provide the public attention and resources necessary to foster human welfare. For instance, if child care is treated as a responsibility for families but not for employers or government, this works to the detriment of children, agents of domestic child care, and the poor. If early child care, including health care, is completely the responsibility of parents, educational and life opportunities for many underprivileged children will be marginal. We now recognize that early childhood experiences can and do have lifelong public consequences in personal, occupational, economic, political, cultural, and educational domains. The position concludes that the impact of public life and policies on what we call private life is so massive and so generally detrimental that categorization of concerns into private and public obscures rather than reveals the important dimensions of such policies in debate and deliberation.

TWO SORTS OF PRIVACY NORMS

The concept of privacy clearly represents different things to different people and, just as clearly, is valued differently. Significantly, two types of social norms structure privacy.

First, some social norms restrict access of others to an individual in a certain domain where the individual is accorded wide discretion concerning how to behave in this domain. A romantic view of the contemporary institution of marriage exemplifies this sort of norm. This sort of privacy promotes private life, individuality, the integrity of various spheres of life, and various associations with people.

Second, social norms can restrict access of others to an individual or to a context but where the behavior carried on in private is rigidly defined by social norms and affords little discretion. Although this sort of behavior is performed in private and is guarded by privacy norms, the point of the norms is not the enhancement of individual choice or expression. For instance, although defecation is a paradigmatically private activity for an adult in our society, there are many ways of managing this activity in private that would be violative of social taboos. The privacy afforded a person for such an activity does not serve the purpose of self-expression; instead, it manifests a rigid and internalized form of social control. The fact that there is little opportunity for directly enforcing the norms should not obscure the point that much of socialization is directed to erecting internal barriers to norm violations.[11] To take another example, there is ample historical evidence that families have functioned and still do function largely as social control mechanisms rather than as refuges from social control.[12] The privacy accorded them enhances the controlling rather than the liberating forces.

One way of gauging this distinction between the two sorts of privacy institutions in the context of the family is to consider whether spouses define themselves primarily by reference to a role or in reference to a relationship. If by a role, there are certain noncontingent patterns of outlook and behavior that are internalized and socially enforced independent of how the other partner behaves.[13]

Suppose that a husband both disregards and mistreats his wife in various serious ways. In some contexts, this would be seen by the wife as a burden but not as a reason to forgo her domestic role or think differently about her responsibilities. These responsibilities are, from her perspective, unconditional. To some extent, and maybe only at the default position, we relate to our children this way. Even if they are unresponsive to supportive overtures and nonreciprocating in love and communication, parents feel they should continue to love their children and to nurture them emotionally.

If the spouses define themselves primarily by a relationship, the way in which one behaves is largely a function of how the other interacts. The relationship is seen as contingent on reciprocity and growth.

In thinking about aged parents of adults, we might find someone expressing the attitude that because his parents were not much help to him when he needed nurturing, he does not owe nurturing to his parents now. This is the relationship perspective. If someone feels he owes his parents care independent of how he was treated, then this exemplifies the role relationship.

Both sorts of norms, the norms that control as well as those that liberate, are privacy norms, typically relate to our practices of showing respect for people and are reflections of social structure and symbolism. But their function in other ways is distinct. As a way of showing respect for people, whether our norms lead us to avert our gaze from others' genitals or feet may well be a matter of convention. As a way of promoting private life and freedom from social control, the means are not as arbitrary. Relaxing the norms that restrict exposure to someone's diary would be more violative of private life than would be a relaxation of norms that restrict exposure of activity on the toilet. The privacy restrictions related to elimination are not designed to afford or facilitate intimate or personal opportunities otherwise not available. The practice of writing a diary aims directly at such opportunities, as I shall illustrate in Chapter 7.

For some people it may be more upsetting and debilitating to be exposed in their bathroom behavior than to be exposed in their diaries. This can be conceded without altering the point about the different roles of these norms in promoting private life.

I mentioned that both sorts of privacy provide means for showing people respect. Hannah Arendt observed that many of the widely shared privacy norms relate to bodily functions that we share with other animals.[14] Stanley Benn has reminded us that these norms often involve notions of shame and impose duties on us not to present certain facets of ourselves in public.[15] This suggests that some of our privacy norms express respect for human dignity by protecting us from public association with the beastly, the unclean. Privacy norms that function to protect human dignity in this way are not protective of individual expression or limitations on social regimentation. Privacy norms that enable private life to transpire by freeing people from social control represent an additional component of human dignity – a component that emerges in certain types of cultural settings.

One type of privacy can evolve into the other. We can think of marital relations as private in the sense that limited exposure norms apply to them even when the behavior in these relations is completely ritualized and allows for no self-expression. Over time, this same institution could evolve into the primary locus of self-expression, still protected by limited exposure norms. I believe that failing to draw this distinction in sorts of privacy norms has hampered our understanding of some central cultural dimensions of privacy.

Max Scheler draws a helpful distinction between two sorts of roles, a distinction that provides insights into what I have been differentiating as roles and relationships. He differentiates roles into those in which individuality is central and those in which it is out of place.[16] Scheler points out how shame can be occasioned when one thinks of himself impersonally in a role but others treat him as personally involved. Being noticed nude by a painter, not as a model, but as something fuller, is Scheler's example. Being treated as an individual rather than as a fungible abstraction leads to a loss of anonymity and, in some contexts, to a loss of self-respect.

This distinction suggests that the way rules operate in impersonal and in personal roles differs dramatically. We can concede that all roles are rule governed, both by the local rules of the practice (i.e., rules governing painters painting models) and by more global moral and social principles (i.e., people should not be murdered or exploited). Nevertheless, those roles that involve us distinctively and emotionally must enable us to feel expressive of ourselves. To allow emotional engagement to arise, roles must be flexible so that people can eventually locate themselves within the role.[17] External scrutiny and regulation can be focused only on the most objective aspects of such roles. Otherwise, inhibitions to fulfillment would abound, as would temptations to redirect the point of the practice to serve public ends. Most significant, roles that involve an individual distinctively and personally are ones in which an individual is emotionally most exposed and vulnerable. This exposure presupposes trust and acceptance of vulnerability. Roles that embrace this trust and vulnerability, and thus permit certain forms of expression and personal development, cannot flourish without privacy of the sort whose norms promote self-expression.

My distinction of two sorts of privacy – one restricting others' access to areas that are nevertheless highly regulated and the other restricting access with the point of allowing for individual expression – has some parallels to the distinction in roles that Scheler articulated. The privacy norms that promote self-expression are those that involve people as fully engaged. I label such roles *expressive roles*. Expressive roles are to be contrasted with more functional roles on the one hand and with restrictions on access that are not aimed at role performance of any sort but reflect social taboos.

The distinction of the two sorts of privacy norms has some bearing on the scope of privacy norms, an issue introduced in the sketch of legal issues. Some would limit privacy to informational or physical access to a person, whereas others regard privacy as encompassing nearly all dimensions of private, personal life. The association of the sort of privacy norms that enable personal expression within dimensions of personal life seems to legitimize the more inclusive interpretations of the scope of privacy. My point is that at the center of one sort of privacy norm is self-expression within a relationship, providing discretion for the agents involved. This range of discretion and expression is not just facilitated by limited access on the part of others. After all, both sorts of privacy norms serve to restrict access to a person. Discretion in self-expression is central to and constitutive of the sort of norm this kind of privacy structures.

PRIVACY AND VULNERABILITY

In earlier sections I related one sort of privacy norm with self-expression, exploration, and vulnerability. Here I want to focus again on the vulnerability element. The root meaning of 'intimate' concerns what is innermost for a person. Those factors in our lives that have highly charged emotions attached to them tend to be what is most intimate and most private. The fact that we have difficulty controlling our emotional reactions in some of these areas suggests that these reactions reflect the real underlying self. As John Sabini and Maury Silver persuasively have argued, our emotional vulnerability, much more than our rationality, makes us fit subjects of moral caring.[18] Moral rules makes sense for us, not only because we are overly calculating in promoting our self-interest, but also because we are potentially out of control, not able to calculate and promote those values that matter.[19]

Richard Wollheim's discussion of inner life in *The Thread of Life*[20] introduces a distinction between the emotional power of an event, actual or imagined, and the cognitive content of thought about that event. Whereas the objective description of an event might be easy to share with another, its emotional impact, one's vulnerability in light of it, may be difficult or inappropriate to convey and for that reason not shared. I had the experience of trying to convey news of a death to other family members and found that I could not speak. Here I could *only* share the emotional power of the death, not the fact of its occurrence. To people who would not share the vulnerability, I had no difficulty in sharing the fact.

We can elaborate on emotional vulnerability as a basis for

privacy by referring to a comment William James makes about secretiveness: "Even where a given habit of concealment is reflective and deliberate, its motive is far less often definite prudence than a vague aversion to having one's sanctity invaded and one's personal concerns fingered and turned over by other people."[21] Metaphors of defilement and pollution to characterize intrusion into personal precincts abound in literature.[22] Innermost aspects of self are supercharged with emotional color. One is defiled if part of this self is wrenched out and exposed as if it were just an ordinary bit of information that means nothing to the world.

PRIVACY AND AUTONOMY

Someone might challenge the line of reasoning that leads to my broad interpretation of privacy with the following counterexample: Whether one is forced into a labor camp or killed is also centrally connected with whether a person will be able to engage in any expressive roles during his life. It does not follow from this that assignment to a labor camp or condemnation to death are infringements of privacy.

The difference between death and access to contraceptives, vis-à-vis privacy, is that while life is a necessary condition for expressive-role activity, it is also a necessary condition for all activity. Access to contraceptives is necessary primarily and specifically for the sort of activity that is peculiarly expressive role–related. Hence it qualifies as falling within the domain of privacy; prohibitions on killing do not. When we look at the political and social debate over the scope of privacy, we will find that this characterization is the one that fits.

Someone can still complain that, as used here, privacy has been conflated with autonomy, with the issue of who has authority to govern a domain of life, whether public or private. Several responses can be suggested. First of all, one does not have to deny that autonomy is relevant to expressive-role domains of life. If we are discussing the borders of privacy and autonomy, it is premature to say that if one category, autonomy, applies, the other does not. Second, if we assume that privacy and autonomy do overlap, because autonomy is the broader concept, it is more informative to describe something in terms of privacy than in terms of autonomy. This informational difference makes it appropriate to depict features of a situation in terms of privacy when both privacy and autonomy apply.[23]

But I think a richer answer to the challenge is possible. Clearly, people need some autonomy in order to engage role-expressive aspects of self. The point of such autonomy, however, is not to disengage the person from the entire web of relations, but to enhance a feature of these relations, to make choices and counterbalances between relationships possible, to afford prospects of deeper relationships. Notions of privacy and intimacy are suggestive of these possibilities. Notions of autonomy, as usually elaborated, are oblivious of it and emphasize instead other, less social dimensions of human direction. (This theme is explored in more detail in Chapter 10.) Privacy, not autonomy, is the appropriate category for conceptualizing expressive-role domains because it situates the domain ultimately in relational ties and not in individualistic boundaries. Both privacy and autonomy suggest that some people have no business crossing a threshold. But in addition to this, privacy suggests that on the other side of that threshold there may be something still interpersonal. The point of the restrictions on access is in large part not to isolate people but to enable them to relate intimately or in looser associations that serve personal and group goals. Characteristically privacy is engaged as a social category not just to preclude a wider influence but to enshroud with respect an association of people that is meaningful in its own terms.

In suggesting that privacy is properly attributed to the domains of personal choice, I do not make any claims about whether the U.S. Constitution affords protection for these domains. My discussion is limited to the issue of whether in ordinary parlance privacy norms appropriately govern certain domains of personal life and personal choice. My con-

21

clusion is that they characteristically do for one sort of privacy norm.

I mentioned in the Introduction that most writing on privacy situates issues of privacy within the context of legal or business affairs. Many of these treatments are excellent, both as illuminating studies and as analyses of statutes and court decisions. There is no need for another review of this literature. To an extent, the traditional focus on privacy as a right to be free of governmental or business intrusion or control may bias our understanding of both privacy and intrusion because of the formulaic rigidity of legal norms and remedies. People have a different relationship to their government and to their societies. Although we can entertain the thought that government is at best a necessary evil, we have a more intimate relationship with our societies and, like all intimate relationships, we have difficulty sorting out what belongs to us and what belongs to the societies of which we are part. I am interested in the role of privacy in the less formal but possibly more important domains of social life, including the whole spectrum of social interaction.[24]

As social beings, we may be more vulnerable to social than to legal coercion, and the strategies that we construct to combat social coercion will be different from those that insulate us from legal coercion. The strategies that protect individuals from the overreaching power of government are mostly dependent on legal remedies. In the social realm, the defenses will have to be of a more nuanced and informal character as represented in social norms. Given the awareness of danger of social control, it is curious (or worse) that so little mainstream philosophical attention is placed on rights and wrongs of social control mechanisms.[25]

The privacy thesis I develop in this book is that privacy norms serve the same function vis-à-vis social coercion that constitutional principles serve vis-à-vis legal coercion, protecting individuals from the overreaching control of others.

Of course, not all constitutional principles protect people from the powerful and not all privacy principles shield people from social pressures. But some do, and when they do, they restrain and channel power. As in the legal sphere, employing principles in the social spheres to protect people presupposes views about what is important about human life and how it is that overreaching on the part of the powerful may derail the normal individual's capacity to locate what is important in his or her life. These views about human life require sensitivity to our potentialities and vulnerabilities – factors that change with historical and cultural circumstances.

Philosophers in particular will find some occupational hurdles in coming to appreciate my suggestions of the way in which privacy functions in social contexts because of their commitment to articulated rationality, to a public standard of evaluation of all aspects of a person's life and being. The standard of articulated rationality has become professionally entrenched regardless of domain: We focus on all areas of concern with the expectation that adequate arguments can be offered for all aspects of one's outlook. Philosophy has not been engaged in an inquisition, forcing people first to reveal and then defend their most personal feelings. Nevertheless, it has assigned to the agent's own conscience the responsibility for revealing and examining all that matters, in light of public standards. This charge can become ruthless and unfeeling if taken literally, and it has sometimes led to advocating exposure of personal intimacies as if these were things a person should be competent to defend before an objective public. I illustrate this potential in Chapter 2 by focusing on John Stuart Mill's treatment of social freedom.

Chapter 2

Mill's approach to social freedom

John Stuart Mill's essay *On Liberty* is motivated by a fervent concern for the rightful limits of social pressure on individuals, and it articulates what these limits should be. Yet Mill's conception of liberty undermines privacy and, in so doing, makes people more rather than less vulnerable to the social control Mill feared. Mill was led to this ironic position through two related misconceptions: an underestimation of the (rightful) effect of the opinions of others on our judgment and behavior and an overestimation of the efficacy of reason, when present, as the governing norm in belief assessment and behavior.

MILL'S CONCERN ABOUT SOCIAL TYRANNY

Mill is expressly concerned with informal or social pressures on individuals to make their lives conform to socially approved models. He notes that social pressures can be more pervasive, unrelenting, and crushing than legal threats and, as a result, do more damage to human personality.

> Society can and does execute its own mandates: and if it issues wrong things with which it ought not to meddle, it practices a social tyranny more formidable than many kinds of political oppression, since, though not usually upheld by such extreme penalties, it leaves fewer means of escape, penetrating much more deeply into the details of life, and enslaving the soul

itself. Protection, therefore, against the tyranny of the mag-
istrate is not enough: there needs protection also against the
tyranny of the prevailing opinion and feeling; against the tendency of society to impose, by other means than civil penalties,
its own ideas and practices as rules of conduct on those who
dissent from them; to fetter the development, and, if possible,
prevent the formation, of any individuality not in harmony
with its ways, and compels all characters to fashion themselves
upon the model of its own.[1]

Mill's distinction here between social pressures that "en-
slave the soul" and legal coercion is important. We intuitively
recognize the difference between giving a person reason to
do something, on the one hand, and structuring the self with
value orientation intact, the seat of judgment, on the other.
Legal coercion works *on* whatever nature the individual has,
channeling its expression along certain courses. Social tyranny, in contrast, distorts the process of development that
makes a self rationally competent and, thereby, enslaves the
soul. A self that is legally coerced can assess its situation. A
self that is socially engineered cannot engage in rational
assessment.

To draw this distinction between subversion and rational
development of a mind, we must have a picture of some
developmental process by which individuals become properly formed. Mill's picture of the process is rather demanding
intellectually, emotionally, and socially. Both the unending
search for reasons and the emotional invulnerability that
characterized Socrates serve as conscious models for Mill's
recipe for rationality.[2]

Recent attention to this question of process has suggested
an interpretation along the following lines: The processes
that develop are ones that enhance our ability to be more
rational – reasons-responsive – rather than less; and the
processes that develop are ones that are stable under discovery – that permit us to endorse them when we understand them.

MILL'S CONFIDENCE IN REASON

Mill's articulation of the conditions of spiritual enslavement is troublesome because of the austere picture of human reason it reflects. Mill differentiates a judgment based on reason from a judgment that stems from other sources of interest, preference, or habit. Especially noteworthy is Mill's stance on what constitutes a rational basis for a social judgment. Unless a person can actually articulate the basis for his or her judgment, the judgment amounts to an expression of mere personal preference, however widely shared that preference may be.[3] This position we shall call the requirement of articulated rationality.

> No one, indeed, acknowledges to himself that his standard of judgment is his own liking; but an opinion on a point of conduct, not supported by reasons, can only count as one person's preference; and if the reasons, when given, are a mere appeal to a similar preference felt by other people, it is still only many people's liking instead of one. To an ordinary man, however, his own preference, thus supported, is not only a perfectly satisfactory reason, but the only one he generally has for any of his notions of morality, taste, or propriety, which are not expressly written in his religious creed; and his chief guide in the interpretation even of that.[4]

One might have thought that a more reasonable position to take would have been one that labeled as a mere preference a view that was controversial in the society to which one persisted in holding despite not having at hand reasons for rejecting alternative outlooks. But for Mill, depicting something as a preference is not limited in this way. However noncontroversial a belief one holds, the fact that everyone else shares it is irrelevant in assessing its status as rational. All that matters is whether one *has* reasons of one's own that one can point to for adopting the belief. We should be reminded that having had at one time reasons for adopting a belief is not the same as having reasons now as, for example, by remembering what those reasons were.[5] Yet it is the ability to defend a belief actively that is required by the principle of articulate rationality, and by Mill.

> The fatal tendency of mankind to leave off thinking about a thing when it is no longer doubtful, is the cause of half their errors.[6]
>
> The Socratic dialectics, so magnificently exemplified in the dialogues of Plato, were a contrivance of this description. They were essentially a negative discussion of the great question of philosophy and life, directed with consummate skill to the purpose of convincing any one who had merely adopted the commonplaces of received opinion that he did not understand the subject – that he as yet attached no definite meaning to the doctrines he professed; in order that, becoming aware of his ignorance, he might be put in the way to obtain a stable belief, resting on a clear apprehension of both the meaning of doctrines and their evidence.[7]

In this passage Mill differentiates merely adopting the commonplaces of received opinion and clear apprehension of the meanings of norms and the evidence for them. If I had to explain why I am more confident about the claim that sex between college faculty and students is a bad idea than I am about the claim that socializing between faculty and students is harmful, I would have to confess, using Mill's criterion, that this difference in confidence constituted a mere preference about what I treated as reliable guidelines. I have very few data about sexual relationships between faculty and students, and what I (and others) have is likely to be skewed toward cases with unhappy outcomes. So in this context, my attitude counts as a mere preference. Significantly, the notion of trusting one's culture in general or as a presumption does not arise for Mill as a basis for rational acceptance of a norm. The norm must be defended to be part of a stock of rationally held attitudes, and the agent who holds the belief must be the one situated to do the defending. We now turn our attention to Mill's formula for prodding adults to be more concerned for the rational grounding of their beliefs.

MILL'S ACCOUNT OF CONFORMISM
AND HIS ACTIVIST ALTERNATIVE

Mill delineates what he takes to be the proper scope and limits of pressures on others to conform.

> The sole end for which mankind are warranted, individually or collectively, in interfering with the liberty of action of any of their number, is self-protection. That the only purpose for which power can be rightfully exercised over any member of a civilized community, against his will, is to prevent harm to others. His own good, either physical or moral, is not a sufficient warrant. He cannot rightfully be compelled to do or forbear because it will be better for him to do so, because it will make him happier, because, in the opinion of others, to do so would be wise or even right. *These are good reasons for remonstrating with him, or reasoning with him, or persuading him, or entreating him, but not for compelling him, or visiting him with any evil in case he do otherwise.*[8]

In this famous passage, Mill sets the threshold of coercion at causing harm to others. Mill does not declare that in self-regarding areas we must pay no attention to other people's conduct or character. On the contrary, as we shall see, he encourages taking an active interest in self-regarding affairs of others. He indicates a range of legitimate responses to self-regarding behavior or habits that people find objectionable in others.

In Chapter 4 of Mill's essay, he begins to articulate the kinds of legitimate pressure individuals or society may employ to reform someone who seems misguided in some of his central, self-regarding life choices. Here I quote several passages illustrating what Mill allows:

> Human beings owe to each other help to distinguish the better from the worse, and encouragement to choose the former and avoid the latter. They should be for ever stimulating each other to increased exercise of their higher faculties, and increased direction of their feelings and aims towards wise instead of

foolish, elevating instead of degrading, objects and contemplations. . . . Considerations to aid his judgment, exhortation to strengthen his will, may be offered to him, even obtruded on him, by others: but he himself is the final judge.[9]

Mill here not only regards it as legitimate, but *makes it mandatory* for people to become actively engaged in improving the self-regarding character traits of others. This is something we "owe to others."

I do not mean that the feelings with which a person is regarded by others ought not to be in any way affected by his self-regarding qualities or deficiencies. This is neither possible nor desirable. . . . There is a degree of folly, and a degree of what may be called (though the phrase is not unobjectionable) lowness or depravation of taste, which, though it cannot justify doing harm to the person who manifests it renders him necessarily and properly a subject of distaste, or, in extreme cases, even of contempt: a person could not have the opposite qualities in due strength without entertaining these feelings. Though doing no wrong to any one, a person may so act as to compel us to judge him, and feel to him, as a fool, or as a being of an inferior order: and since this judgment and feeling are a fact which he would prefer to avoid, it is doing him a service to warn him of it beforehand, as of any other disagreeable consequence to which he exposes himself. *It would be well, indeed, if this good office were much more freely rendered than the common notions of politeness at present permit, and if one person could honestly point out to another that he thinks him in fault, without being considered unmannerly or presuming.*[10]

Mill is explaining that institutions of social manners interfere with fitting gestures to inform others of our low regard conjoined with instruction as to how they can improve in our estimation of them. Inhibiting precepts of social manners should be abandoned.

Mill then proceeds to caution about the subtle but important distinction between naturally responding to another's offensiveness and socially punishing a person.

We have a right, also, in various ways, to act upon our unfavorable opinion of any one, not to the oppression of his
individuality, but in the exercise of ours. We are not bound,
for example, to seek his society; we have a right to avoid it
(though not to parade the avoidance). . . . We have a right, and
it may be our duty, to caution others against him, if we think
his example or conversation likely to have a pernicious effect
on those with whom he associates. We may give others a
preference over him in optional good offices, except those
which tend to his improvement. In these various modes a
person may suffer very severe penalties at the hands of others
for faults which directly concern only himself; but he suffers
these penalties only in so far as they are the natural, and, as
it were, the spontaneous consequences of the faults themselves, not because they are purposely inflicted on him for the
sake of punishment. . . .

What I contend for is, that the inconveniences which are
strictly inseparable from the unfavorable judgment of others,
are the only ones to which a person should ever be subject for
that portion of his conduct and character which concerns his
own good, but which does not affect the interests of others in
their relations with him.

We may reprimand or avoid a person we find distasteful,
or we may warn others of a person's odiousness. What we
may not do is inflict social injury on him because we judge
him wanting. We may regard him as disqualified from many
associations, but we may not try to inflict harm that is not
the natural result of his self-regarding behavior.

In standard treatments of punishment, we find authors
differentiating the harm to a violator that is the natural consequence of his behavior from the purposeful infliction of
harm on a person because of his wrong. Thus, a person who
drives under the influence of alcohol, smashes his car into a
light pole, and loses his sight as a result is not said strictly
to be punished by this loss. Rather, the only punishment
proper that this drunk driver receives is what is intentionally
inflicted on him by people whose objective is to deprive the
offender of some good because of what he did.[11]

This distinction becomes much more difficult to apply in

the social realm, where formal punishments are not set out and where differences between natural consequences and intentional infliction are subtle. In the social realm, if we dissociate ourselves from a person because of that person's habits or character, we are acting as we have a right to act and as having standards requires us to act. But we may do more. We may warn others and confront the individual with our own assessment of that person's invidious nature. We may ignore the contemporary standards of politeness and offer people a sincere and well-meaning assessment of our regard for them. The problem is that only a fine line prevents these tactics from evolving into intimidation and harassment, particularly when one's own critical assessment is widely shared. Oddly, in an area where one might have thought a great deal of subtlety would be needed to be protective of people's individuality, Mill unleashes an activism that has no limitation in scope. Anything about another's life becomes open game for our probing challenges. So long as we are armed with our rational arguments and aim at nursing some improvement to character, we may confront another with our concern. Whereas we might say to others that challenge us in some self-regarding domain of life, that what they are concerning themselves with is none of their business, Mill would strip us of the shield of privacy. His reasoning is that privacy stands in the way of challenges that generate rational improvement.

MILL ON THE RIGHT TO RESENTMENT

In the social arena, Mill differentiates punishment from natural consequences of an act or a trait, by reference to moral emotions.

> The distinction between the loss of consideration which a person may rightly incur by defect of prudence or of personal dignity, and the reprobation which is due to him for an offence against the rights of others is not a merely nominal distinction. It makes a vast difference both in our feelings and in our

conduct toward him whether he displeases us in things in which we think we have a right to control him, or in things we know that we have not.[12]

Mill instructs us that we are not wronged by people bungling their personal affairs because we had no right or vested interest that they conform to our expectation. Others do not owe *us* lives loaded with personal virtues, and thus we have limited grounds for complaint concerning failures that primarily affect their lives.[13] There is no suggestion here that the self-regarding virtues are not important or even as important as the other-regarding virtues, for Mill says explicitly that they are. It is only that the fact of their importance does not entitle us to certain means to remedy the situation.

Mill would not permit us to create criminal sanctions for behavior that is low, imprudent, or loathsome as long as it is primarily self-regarding. He would criticize our feeling resentment, or our seeking social retribution, toward those we know who exemplify such a low but self-regarding pattern. Still, we are permitted to make such self-regarding factors of character our business and remonstrate with those we find defective in ways that do not affect others. As we have seen, Mill suggested that we would even be well advised to lower the threshold of restraint that must be passed before we are socially at liberty to point out to people the ways in which self-regarding aspects of their lives fall short of what we take to be the right ideal. The extent to which people are answerable to self-selected others for their self-regarding behavior is heightened in Mill's account. The means people may use to augment the behavior of others is more limited, excluding intentional infliction of social harm. However, the range of behavior that is an apt topic for social influence is extended, perhaps considerably, over current standards. Ironically, in liberating people from criminal and socially punitive sanctions as well as from the sentiment of resentment for self-regarding behavior, Mill exposed them to social confrontation in a way that may intensify the social control that concerned Mill so profoundly, and against which

32

his treatise on liberty was written. Recall what he said about the tyranny of social pressure: "It leaves fewer means of escape, penetrating much more deeply into the details of life, and enslaving the soul itself."[14]

What emotional and cognitive defenses would a person have against the social forces Mill unleashes? There will be two sorts of cases to consider: first, where the person displaying socially nonconforming tendencies has adopted such tendencies as a result of extensive thought and argument and, second, where the person has adopted such tendencies not because of some reasoned judgment but because it seems to fit his own nature, independent of whether it is better than the social norm. An example of the first is that a person paints her house with a color that clashes with the neighboring houses because paints that do not clash are discovered to be toxic. An example of the second is that a person paints her house in a silly pattern because it strikes her fancy to have something ridiculous standing on the street.

A CRITIQUE

There is something missing in Mill's sensitivity to the issue of social freedom. Mill argues that, in self-regarding areas of life, the individual is to be afforded complete discretion. Exercising this discretion is the peculiar calling of a human life. Finally, he believes that legal and social punishments are not appropriate tools for directing how this discretion is exercised. In those areas where others have no right to a particular exercise of directed action, we must respect the individual's right to his or her own resolution. But respecting this right does not preclude confronting this person with our assessment.

In fairness to Mill, it is important to put into context some of these positions. First, Mill is not quite declaring open season on social misfits. In his discussion of individual rights to liberty, he points out how few people know a person's situation well enough to assess what is really good for another person. He also warns of the danger of doing more harm than good by interfering with another in self-regarding matters. Finally, Mill surely would endorse the position that even well-meant advice is gratuitous and potentially harmful in many contexts. Even granting all this, however, it remains the case that for Mill, the position that some matter is not anyone else's business is not a fortress behind which one can seek shelter. Mill has simply discarded a whole department in the institution of privacy and thereby exposed people to social pressures to account for themselves and to conform to others' expectations.

We can explain Mill's outlook by reference to his faith in reason – his confidence that understanding the role of argument liberates us, immunizes us, from unworthy influences. The general idea is that if we either understand things well ourselves or if we realize that we are dealing in an area of mere preference we will feel no pressure from those who see things differently. We cannot be as sanguine about the effects of rational inquiry as was Mill. Studies in the socialization of scientists and other professionals suggest a different picture entirely of what reasoning involves.[15] We now think of rational inquiry as a social practice that depends for its accomplishment on faithful transmission of accepted truths and procedures for validation. The principle of articulated rationality, taken seriously, leaves one without foundation. In Chapter 5, I shall argue that our tendency to model ourselves on others around us is not the virus that philosophers, following Mill, argue infects our capacity for responsible thought and action. But as a first point of criticism, we can say that Mill's vision of the use of reason is insufficiently grounded in social practice, excessively individualistic, and demanding on the resources of any person seeking justification. I shall go on to discuss a second problem with Mill's estimate of reason: its emotional and cognitive effectiveness outside a system of social support.

Although Mill worried that people fail their own nature under the pressures of conformity, he underrated the positive role conforming impulses play in people's lives. We shall focus on the constructive role of conformity and the value of so-

cial pressure in Chapter 5. Rather than finding the tension between conforming and individualistic tendencies creative and
essential, Mill argued as if rationalistic and individualistic tendencies were themselves sufficient to generate both individual and social flourishing. Rather than regarding social
pressure as a sometimes legitimate factor in human interaction, Mill rather one-dimensionally would restrict efforts at
influencing people to rational argumentation and the natural
consequences of people finding merit in different arguments.

As a practical matter, we cannot afford to forswear forms
of influencing people that are not cognitively directed. We
know that expressions of support, encouragement, and caring, on the one hand, and disapproval, contempt, and criticism, on the other, are important factors in our own
behavior. We are not so confident in our own judgment and
motivation to think that we should be immune from such
forces all the time, even though strictly they do not appeal
to rational grounds of belief or conviction.

Because I consider the constructive role of social pressure
in more detail in Chapter 6, just a word or two here will
suffice to show that there is a problem with Mill's approach
to social influence. To use an example that Mill discussed,
consider the person who is an alcoholic. We know that al-
coholics have a better chance of abstaining from excessive
drinking if they are situated in a context of support and caring
than in one of indifference or encouragement to drink alcohol. Should we forgo this information in dealing with people with drinking problems because appeal to these forms of
social approval is not the provision of a reason not to drink?
Should we revile the use of role models to help direct *normal
adults* in directions that we think more responsible, even in
self-regarding domains, because again the example is not a
reason, but a form of social pressure?

What we call reason alone we know often not to be an
effective motivator. What is more commonly effective is concern over what others will think of them and people's sense
of how they fit in.

Some (I guess Hegelians) would argue that the important

social norms embody (some semblance of) reason's demands and place these in a context so that they will have maximal behavioral impact. Socialization would direct the whole range of human resources to the objective of getting people to live by certain values. Could we want to be or live among people indifferent to such nonrational factors?

The proper response to social overreaching is not reconstruction of the individual. Mill did not seem to appreciate how individuals or institutions actually work. In light of this, his recommendations carry little force. Instead of engineering individuals to be socially indifferent, we would do well to focus on reconstituting social forms so that the value imperialism that Mill feared from mass society is restricted to its proper realm.

If there is going to be a democratic ideal, it will have to be one more accessible to people as they are, and its measure of achievement will have to be more modest and less demanding than Mill's. A good candidate for this democratic goal is the option of real participation in multiple and alternative associations, sets of spheres of expression and involvement that are specific to domains of life. A system of distributed or individualized and/or privatized goals, each with its own social support mechanism, is clearly less formidable and requires less robustness on the part of citizens than the sort of independence Mill recommends. The more associations or communities the individual can choose among, the less any one community will be effective at imposing its values, and the more the identification of values will seem to be at the individual's discretion. The greater number of differently directed associations in which a person participates, the less vulnerable the individual is vis-à-vis any particular association. As I argue in several chapters of this book, such recommendations for managing human social dependence better reflect what we know about individual and social processes. The institution of privacy is a key element in maintaining the independence of associations, affording people the sort of freedom from social control that initially motivated Mill to write *On Liberty*.

Chapter 3

Articulated rationality and the Archimedean critique of culture

We saw in our discussion of Mill that reasoning in general and moral reasoning in particular were individuated and distrustful of culture. Culture lulled one into accepting as inevitable principles that should be challenged. Because only one's own reasoning is to be trusted, each person has the responsibility of constructing morality. Otherwise people just "parrot" received truths and betray their own nature. (Nothing comparable with Euclid's *Elements* is available to guide one on social and moral matters.)

This approach to moral reasoning generates a problem of how one is connected with other people. Any connection has to be constructed from within the theory rather than taken as a given. The process of constructing whatever connection is there strongly disposes, if not forces, the person to seek an answer in terms that in the first instance appeal to individualized values. Culture and connections with others, if valuable, are valuable because of what they offer the individual. Relations with others thereby theoretically are relegated to a dependent or secondary importance.

As it did in the case of Mill, this approach disposes one to regard social pressures as inappropriate and rationally corrupting. This disposition in turn promotes misunderstanding the role of privacy in the regulation of life and in its relationship to social freedom. Mill, recall, treated regard for a person's privacy as diminishing a person's opportunities for critical and helpful assessment by others in self-regarding domains of life. Social freedom for Mill was achieved when two conditions were met, one social and one individual: Society must be structured so as not to punish people for self-regarding idiosyncrasies; the individual judges and acts on the basis of reasons rather than concern with what others think.

Mill is wrong in his analysis of rationality, privacy, and social freedom. Mill is wrong in his assessment of the relationship of culture and morality, and it is primarily this latter mistake that leads to the others – specifically to a misunderstanding of the relations between privacy and morality and between privacy and social freedom.

The elements of Mill's outlook that stand in the way of a better understanding include his view of the relationship between morality and culture, and his view of the nature and limits of human judgment. Much of contemporary analytic moral theory shares these elements of Mill's outlook, and this in turn shapes our perspective of what morality is about. Yet morality is not about any of the list of things usually identified by philosophers; in fact, the assumptions about reasoning made in much moral theory are wrong in a way that has significant consequences. In the present chapter, I illustrate how widely shared Mill's view about the relationship of culture and morality is and offer some reasons for thinking that this outlook is not inescapable. By becoming clearer about the interdependence of morality and culture, we can better understand the place of social pressure for both social control and social freedom, and privacy's role in modulating this force.

CONFORMISM

Conformity gets bad press. It has neither the romance nor the heroism associated with liberal individualism. It is regarded as a threat to autonomy of thought and action. Our generation is witness to the actualized potential of conformism to generate mindless adherence to catastrophic ends. Not surprisingly, numerous strands in contemporary social criticism adopt the perspective and ideals Mill endorsed, particularly in their treatment of conforming impulses.

David Riesman analyzes the dangers of a culture given over to conformity.[1] According to him, our age makes us particularly vulnerable to such pressures. In a period like ours, where there is so much economic interdependence and so little that differentiates the competing providers of the social and natural goods, a comparatively large emphasis must be placed on anticipating public perception. To survive in this context, we must cater to this common outlook, and reform ourselves, our services, or our products in a way that is attuned to consumers' demands in both social and economic transactions. The peculiar asset of those who succeed in our culture is accommodation to the forever shifting demands of style in public standards. Such a condition for achievement has an important impact on social rationality, requiring a fluidity in both personal and institutional organizations that matches the arrhythmic play of social outlooks. Success is defined in terms of social satisfaction. The virtue that befits this condition is hypersensitivity to the public perspective. We live with an anxiety that we will not be what others seek, because we lack inner-directed values that might have compensated us when confronting social disappointments and that might have afforded us a sense of authenticity. People oriented to life in this way are labeled "other-directed" by Riesman.

> What is common to all other-directeds is that their contemporaries are the source of direction for the individual – either who is known to him or those with whom he is indirectly acquainted, through friends and through mass media. This source is of course "internalized" in the sense that dependence on it for guidance in life is implanted early. The goals toward which the other-directed person strives shift with that guidance: it is only the process of striving itself and the process of paying close attention to the signals from others that remain unaltered throughout life.[2]

Privacy and social freedom

Reminiscent of Mill's concerns about the effectiveness of mass opinion and pressure is Riesman's argument that our own culture equips us with a criterion of self-worth that is nearly exclusively gauged in terms of approval by others.

> Much of our ideology – free enterprise, individualism, and all the rest – remains competitive and is handed down by parents, teachers, and the mass media. At the same time there has been an enormous ideological shift favoring submission to the group, a shift whose decisiveness is concealed by the persistence of the older ideological patterns. The peer-group becomes the measure of all things; the individual has no defenses the group cannot batter down. In this situation the competitive drives for achievement sponsored in children by the remnants of inner-direction in their parents come into conflict with the cooperative demands sponsored by the peer-group. The child therefore is forced to rechannel the competitive drive for achievement, as demanded by the parent, into his drive for approval from the peers.[3]

An interesting depiction of one way in which conforming patterns are maintained is outlined in another study of the dangers of conformity as follows:

> In studies of social clubs and other small groups, conformity pressures have frequently been observed. Whenever a member says something that sounds out of line with the group's norms, the other members at first increase their communication with the deviant. Attempts to influence the nonconformist member to revise or tone down his dissident ideas continue as long as most members of the group feel hopeful about talking him into changing his mind. But if they fail after repeated attempts, the amount of communication they direct toward the deviant decreases markedly. The members begin to exclude him, often quite subtly at first and later more obviously, in order to restore the unity of the group.[4]

Validating Mill's judgment that social pressure is more insidious than legal coercion, because of the way the former

40

immobilizes judgment, recent studies paint the following picture:

> In a cohesive group of policy-makers the danger is not that each individual will fail to reveal his strong objections to a proposal favored by the majority but that he will think the proposal is a good one, without attempting to carry out a critical scrutiny that could lead him to see that there are grounds for strong objections. When groupthink dominates, suppression of deviant thought takes the form of each person's deciding that his misgivings are not relevant, that the benefit of any doubt should be given to the group consensus. A member of a cohesive group will rarely be subjected to direct group pressures from the majority because he or she will rarely take a position that threatens the unity of the group.[5]

The "concurrence-seeking tendency . . . fosters overoptimism, lack of vigilance, and sloganistic thinking about the weakness and immorality of out-groups."[6] This can lead to dehumanizing actions directed at those who are not part of one's group, or even to dehumanizing attitudes toward parts of oneself that are not endorsed by *the group*. It is easy to find examples of situations where pressures to conform outlook and behavior come to undermine the purpose for which the association was initiated.[7]

We are molded and directed by our culture, and we are influenced by peer-group attitudes. The question cannot be whether these social processes are formative but rather when they overstep their proper bounds. Our ideals, our values, our practices, our circumstances, our history, our prospects – all of these enter into the process of settling the proper level of influence of our peers and culture on us.[8]

For Riesman, as for Mill, it matters not just what our values are, but also how we come to hold them. If we see self-formation as a passive process, the freedom to be one way rather than another does not count for much. And this goes for all the characterological forms that Riesman describes. If Riesman is right about what happens to language and public rationality in an other-directed society, we are not competent to differentiate rational from merely effective argumentation. We have become consumers of language and rationality in the same way and for the same other-directed reasons that we have become consumers of other commodities: They fit the social expectations.

The challenges posed by our conforming dispositions must be addressed. They are inadequately addressed by efforts to eliminate the disposition completely. There are several reasons for this. First, as we will see in later chapters, important components of our moral and social capacities are attributable to these tendencies. Recognizing this is critical for understanding morality. Second, the alternative of rationally constructing moral life without reference to cultural perspectives does not offer a plausible grounding for the outlooks and institutions that are central to moral life. In emphasizing the problems with counterconformist approaches, I do not intend to downplay the problems with conformity. Instead, I aim to assure appreciation of a more nuanced approach to the whole question of rationality and conformity – an approach that does not admit of patterned or decontextualized resolutions. An elaboration of some culturally hostile motifs in contemporary moral theory will help show why such a shift in emphasis is necessary.

THE CULTURAL SKEPTICISM OF MORAL THEORY

Philosophers acknowledge that having a moral theory is not a necessary condition for behaving morally.[9] Nevertheless, from the standard philosophical perspective, *something* worthwhile is missing from the ordinary outlook. This missing element is an understanding of what morality is about and how it fixes features of moral reasoning and truth (in case there is a truth to morals in the theory). Theory's function is to furnish these missing elements.[10] Characteristically, this missing element of the ordinary outlook is *not* just of theoretical import but is connected to an agent's capacity to exhibit the all-important moral virtue, autonomy. Laurence Thomas fairly represents this outlook:

For [the morally nonautonomous], right behavior consists in doing one's duty, showing respect for authority, and maintaining the given social order. Their moral views are strongly influenced by social institutions. Indeed, they are not prepared to put too much distance between their own moral views and those of their fellow citizen (or the group of individuals with whom they identify). In fact, the morally nonautonomous are quite concerned that their own moral views meet with social approval; accordingly, they are prepared to alter them in the face of widespread disapproval. The morally nonautonomous are concerned minimally, if at all, with being able to offer justificatory reasons for their moral views and behavior.[11]

As I will illustrate here, an important approach within moral theory threatens to unseat convention, authority, and tradition as a basis of judgment, finding in them corrupting or distorting influences. Theory addresses, in part, the question of what qualities of an act make it right or virtuous, or what qualities of a state or character make it good. In almost no theory is the proper answer to this basic question to be cashed out in terms of convention, authority, or tradition. Indeed, these are, as we saw with Mill, the forces that stand in the way of clear moral thinking. Enlightenment is achieved when convention and authority are completely replaced by reflections that each individual can personally validate. Kant expresses this outlook as follows:

Enlightenment is man's emergence from his self-imposed immaturity. Immaturity is the inability to use one's understanding *without guidance from another*. . . . Rules and formulas, those mechanical aids to the rational use, or rather misuse of his natural gifts, are the shackles of a permanent immaturity.[12]

Because of this attitude toward culture or reliance on the judgments of those around one, modern theorists have found it critical to look to moral theory to provide something both autonomous of culture and grounded on some culturally uncontaminated notion of reason and reflection on experience. To the extent that theory can satisfy this expectation, it perfectly fulfills the requirements of the principle of rational articulation already introduced in connection with John Stuart Mill.

It is sobering to realize the extent to which much philosophical ethics adopts the posture that to be culturally situated is to be morally and rationally corrupted. Much of moral philosophy completely discounts the species character, the historical character, of the human mind. According to the dominant approach, exemplified in the positions of Kant and Mill, it is only by discarding our cultural blinders and our cognitive interdependence that we can adequately progress to clarity and truth. An essential feature of this approach is the view that each individual is competent to assess and validate the entire moral structure. I label this philosophical conceit the *Prometheus complex*, because it purports to supply the light by which humans can transcend their limited condition. It is comparable with the position that only by eliminating traditional outlooks can one achieve scientific understanding.

I connect this philosophical conceit with an attitude about the role of modern scientific inquiry in providing nearly every kind of understanding humans need. Claude Lévi-Strauss states:

> The fact that modern science dates back only a few centuries raises a problem which ethnologists have not sufficiently pondered. The Neolithic Paradox would be a suitable name for it. It was in neolithic times that man's mastery of the great arts of civilization – of pottery, weaving, agriculture and the domestication of animals – became firmly established. No one today would any longer think of attributing these enormous advances to the fortuitous accumulation of a series of chance discoveries or believe them to have been revealed by the passive perception of certain natural phenomena.[13]

The attitude that moral theory enables us to minimize the influence of culture is well represented in preeminent contemporary contributions. In *A Theory of Justice*,[14] Rawls recommends that we identify the underlying principles for social organization only after stripping ourselves of any specific cultural or historical understanding. Such information is excluded, in part, because it is thought to bias and render illegitimate any conclusion based on it. The principles we should agree to are ones that we would accept if we thought about ourselves as heads of families bereft of any specific conception of a just society or of a good life. Rather than conform to prior expectations of the good or the right, we are taken to be looking for principles with which others might reasonably be expected to agree. This approach manifests the Kantian attitude of relegating to culture the pathological role of pollutant or corruptor of moral sensibilities. The constructive aspects of Rawls's powerful theory preclude us from advancing any principles in the original position because we think them right. Instead, right itself requires independent validation and comes to mean something like: would be agreed to in the original position.[15]

For Rawls, as for Kant, the principles that an autonomous person is to live by cannot be validated by reference to any contingent features of the particular society of which he or she is part. For both Kant and Rawls, it is not even one's participation in a social structure that establishes one's moral nature, but rather one's freedom, equality, and rationality.[16] Explicitly, Rawls takes the *mutual disinterest* of the parties in the original position to be a key feature of his own and Kant's understanding of autonomy. Our nature is best expressed when we act on principles that free, equal, mutually disinterested beings would adopt in the original position.[17] We discern from this last point that it is not our social nature that expresses what is most esteemed in us but our independence and rational competence. Social disengagement reflects for Rawls, and for nearly the whole contract tradition, what is morally deepest about people.[18] I return to this point in Chapter 5 when I discuss an alternative picture of what is basic to moral understanding.

It is true that Rawls uses this apparatus to develop a rich and inspired vision of the individual good as bound up with social sharing, in which life in common is experienced as an end in itself. The point, though, is that social identification has to be fashioned for Rawls while the disengagement is taken as given. The value of society has to be constructed for disengaged selves. In other contexts, such disengaged selves would be classified as suffering from a sociopathic personality disorder. Why isn't it that the value of disengagement has to be established for engaged selves?

Jon Elster suggests an answer to this question of primacy. He says that it is possible to imagine a world in which each person is motivated exclusively by selfish concerns, but it is not possible to imagine a world in which people are motivated by exclusively altruistic concerns.[19] How can your only goal be to help someone whose only goal is to help you? Elster argues that the lack of grounding for reciprocated dependence shows that for methodological reasons we must assume that selfish individual motivations are primary.

This methodological argument is spurious. First of all, if it is possible for one person to have as an exclusive goal helping someone else, then it is possible for a second person to have as an exclusive goal helping someone whose exclusive goal is helping the first person. Neither agent has a foothold to action, but that is a different point, unrelated to motivation, and it is motivation that is at issue.

A second problem with Elster's account has to do with interpreting what is meant by altruistic motivation. Suppose a young child upon hearing another child wail in distress brings an adult to help the pained child. Must there be a selfish individual motivation behind the call for help? Couldn't there even be an evolutionary explanation for altruistic motivations not grounded on selfish reasons?

A third problem with Elster's argument is that it assumes that altruistic motivations are guided by what other agents want rather than by what is good for them. There is nothing incoherent in my being solely motivated by, say, assuring that you are healthy, and you being solely motivated by improving my understanding. You spend your time explaining things to me, and I spend my time planning your diet, exercise, and so forth. My goal of helping you does not have

46

to internally represent your goal of helping me in the way Elster suggests.

Annette Baier, in contrast to Jon Elster and John Rawls, argues that from a methodological perspective, the standard way of representing what is basic as something unsocial is misguided. She shows that trust and social sharing are pre-supposed in, not established through, all the moral constructions.

> Since the things we typically do value include such things as we cannot singlehandedly either create or sustain (our own life, health, reputation, our offspring and their well-being, as well as intrinsically shared goods, . . . and so on) we must allow many other people to get into positions where they can, if they choose, injure what we care about, since those are the same positions that they must be in in order to help us take care of what we care about. The simple Socratic truth that no person is self-sufficient gets elaborated, once we add the equally So-cratic truth that the human soul's activity is *caring* for things into the richer truth that no one is able by herself to look after everything she wants to have looked after, nor even alone to look after her own "private" goods, such as health and bodily safety.[20]

Later in the same essay, Baier drives home the point that we cannot plausibly find voluntarist or explicit contractual solutions to the problem of needing to trust and to care for others:

> Trust can come with no beginnings, with gradual as well as sudden beginnings, and with various degrees of self-consciousness, voluntariness, and expressness. My earlier discussion of the delicacy and tact needed by the truster in judging the performance of the trusted applied only to cases where the truster not merely realizes that she trusts but has some conscious control over the continuation of the trust relation-ship. The discussion of abuses of discretionary power applied only to cases where the truster not merely realizes that she trusts but has some conscious control over the continuation of the trust relationship. But trust relationships need not be so

express, and some important forms of them cannot be verbally acknowledged by the persons involved. Trust between infant and parent is such a case.[21]

We find ourselves situated and engaged in caring about common and overlapping ends. Baier points out that caring about the same things provides the best reasons for confidence in another's cooperation and trust. The disengaged stance that is adopted in some pivotal moral theories is not the inevitable starting point, either methodologically or substantively.

The injunction of articulate rationality arises in evaluations of both particular norms and the susceptibility to internalize what one sees others do and profess. Rather than being part of social and individual rationality, such susceptibility precludes rationality for Mill, Rawls, and others I shall soon discuss. The reason this susceptibility precludes rationality is not based on the presumption that the society is immoral, but on the presumption that no objective defense of the cultural norms will be accessible to people who are its participants. This means that there is a fundamental conflict between the autonomy engendering restriction on reasons that much of philosophical theory requires and the disposition to be a socially attuned being.

Before I cite other examples of moral philosophers' attitude toward rational validation of morality, it would be worthwhile to specify several strands that are woven together in this perspective. First, it is our rational nature that underlies our moral character. Second, because rational nature so characteristically is conceived in terms of means–end efficiency,[22] we have ends natural to our human character that are best achieved through moral strategies, so that our moral or social character is a means to the fulfillment of some independently definable end. This end may be affected by the means employed, but still this socially disengaged end is fundamental. Third, for us to manifest our nature fully, we must renounce any appeal to how the culture or people generally conceive of addressing the problems that we confront in life. Validation must be personal, or else we are not genuinely expressing our source of dignity.

Another influential argument reminiscent of Mill's position is provided by Ronald Dworkin.[23] Dworkin differentiates two senses of morality, the critical sense and the descriptive sense. Morality in the descriptive sense is not an appropriate basis for coercive social policy according to Dworkin. Relying on descriptive morality violates democratic scruples that individuals should not be restricted without certain sorts of reasons applying. Facts about how others see and wish to continue to see the social world fail to provide an adequate basis for such restrictions.

Critical morality, in contrast, is morality that is amenable to certain sorts of defense, making reference "to some . . . small set of very general standards," that because of their abstract character will vary little from person to person.[24] If the belief of others that the behavior in question is immoral is the only basis a person can offer for claiming something as a moral truth, then the person is not in possession of a real moral conviction but is merely parroting, as Mill would put the point. A person must have his or her own reasons for thinking that something is wrong, even though the reasons might have been taught to the agent by others.[25]

It is instructive to see what Dworkin does in the case of an appeal to religious teachings as the basis for a moral assessment. Dworkin would allow this appeal, provided the person can consistently defend the difference between legitimate and illegitimate appeals to religious doctrines. For instance, for one who does not accept all commands in the Bible as valid, if the appeal is to biblical requirements, one jmust be able to show why this requirement, but not all biblical requirements, is authoritative.

Dworkin, like Mill, is searching for some criterion to distinguish moral convictions from emotional reactions. Surely there is such a distinction, but one might question everything about Dworkin's account of the difference. A man who believes that incest with his adolescent daughter or granddaughter is wrong, and who can only point to the common norm or even to taboos to explain his view is nevertheless expressing a moral conviction. A person who believes, but cannot prove, Herbrand's Theorem nevertheless believes a logical truth, and if he is sincere, his belief amounts to a conviction. If this person is like most of us, his belief *is* a parroting of what logicians tell us. The distinction between a moral position and an emotional reaction has little to do with a person's ability to defend the belief rationally. And perhaps there is no decision that differentiates moral from nonmoral beliefs.

It is worthwhile to contrast Dworkin's reasoning about morality, on the one hand, with his reasoning about adjudication on the other.[26] Whereas principled adjudication is bound by precedent, critical morality is bound by no institutional, conventional, or historical constraints. Indeed, Dworkin points out in a recent essay that typically any explicit allusions to a conventional foundation of ethics, taken to include "convictions about which types of lives are good or bad for a person to lead," are at odds with normal beliefs about the basis for that perspective.[27] That is to say, people do not believe that a community's endorsement of a moral position is the sort of thing that can make the position right. Dworkin is clear about which factors play no part in his account of critical morality. I am unaware of any more positive statement of what legitimately serves as a basis for critical morality.

In an elegantly argued paper on communitarian bases for moral judgment, Jeremy Waldron also demarcates community values from critical morality.[28] Waldron argues throughout the essay that providing a rational defense is central to *our* understanding of what it is to offer a position as a moral position. The terms of this defense must be drawn, Waldron claims, from "the idea of individual fulfillment and the respect people owe one another." Waldron even claims that one cannot be engaged in serious moral thought unless this thought is predicated on the "fundamental equality of human worth."[29] (To what status of moral thinker does this criterion relegate Aristotle?) Without disagreeing about this as an ideal, one is hard put to find in Waldron or other writers a critical defense of this principle. And this from writers who insist on articulate rationality as a precondition of moral judgment proper.

Waldron criticizes communitarians for the incoherence implicit in recognizing something as simultaneously moral and rooted in particular community values. But when articulating his own liberal philosophical position, he recognizes that we are stuck, when challenged, with realizing and announcing that this is where we stand. This response hardly sounds like a critical defense of a position that Waldron and so many others regard as definitive of moral judgment. Nor does it clarify how the liberal or individualist's position differs from the conservative or communitarian position on this fundamental issue of transcending provincialism.

To offer one more notable and explicit example of the Prometheus complex, I offer this passage from Richard Brandt:

> Our normative beliefs are strongly affected by the particular cultural tradition which tutored us, and would be different if we had been in a learning situation with different parents, teachers, or peers. . . . What we should aim to do is step outside our own tradition somehow, see it from the outside, and evaluate it, separating what is only the vestige of a possibly once useful moral tradition from what is justifiable at present.[30]

Cultural norms for Brandt are undependable guides to morally correct positions. They are also constitutionally incapable of critical self-assessment. Brandt offers no argument that evaluation from within a cultural tradition is ineffective in weeding out problems or that evaluation from outside a tradition is even possible.

The examples assembled here illustrate a position common to philosophical and more broadly cultural criticism. If we view our culture as an alternative to morality, and as a deficient one at that, then it must rest with individual resources, particularly those resources validated as free from cultural contamination, to demarcate the aims and structure of moral life. Our rationality should satisfy the principle of articulated rationality.

Moral theory, as I mentioned, aims at illuminating what morality is about. For the utilitarian, its essence is human happiness. For the contractarian, its essence is addressing others with the same respect that we would expect from them. For the Kantian, its essence is rational autonomy. For some, its essence is facilitating solutions to prisoner's dilemma problems. While each of these items is morally worthy and important, none of them really connects us in an essential way with other people or with aspects of ourselves that we esteem, except when we are engaging in abstract philosophy. Something critical is missing from these pictures. As I argue later, this missing factor is just the element that moral theory traditionally aims to eradicate: our dependence on other people within the context of a shared way of life. Thus it is no coincidence that standard representations of social freedom will find conforming tendencies subversive. Nor is it a coincidence that standard representations of privacy will stress individual boundaries rather than relational features of life.

My aim in this chapter is to show that the attitude toward culture that Mill expressed is representative of contemporary theory as well. The problems of connecting morality with culture and of people with people become evident in this approach. These problems in turn obscure our understanding of the role of social pressure, the meaning of social freedom, and the role privacy plays. In the next chapter, I discuss what is known about our rational independence in the cognitive and the moral domains. To the extent to which influential moral theories misconceive how humans work cognitively and socially, the theories are in need of adjustment.

Chapter 4

Social freedom from the perspective of cognitive and social psychology

Our understanding of privacy and the role it plays in structuring social freedom is the focus of this book. Obscuring our view of these concepts are confidence in a narrow notion of rationality and a corresponding denigration of culture and conforming tendencies in the properly formed moral consciousness. Evidence of this confidence and denigration appears in the preceding two chapters.

In those chapters, I illustrate the pervasiveness, if not the overall dominance, of a view of how moral judgment relates to cultural norms. According to that picture, cultural norms have no moral authority and only coincidental relevance. Independent validation of a norm is construed narrowly to require that one employ the principle of articulated rationality with reference to that norm. As I explained, this principle has two elements: (1) that one is not in a proper state vis-à-vis one's beliefs and values unless one is in possession of a rational defense of these principles and (2) that reference to what one's culture or community accepts is not part of a rational defense. The individual is judged competent to find compelling reasons of the right sort on which to construct a moral outlook. For the outlook to be successfully grounded, it should appeal to an individual with no preexisting allegiance to a community norm as such. For us to express our nature fully, we must renounce any appeal to how the cultures around us influence us. To tolerate the influence of a culture on our judgment of what is right is to bias the evaluation and undermine the critical role reasoning can play.

In this chapter, I argue that critical features of rational articulation do not mesh with cognitive and social studies of how people operate. I show that our standard view as to what goes into a moral or social judgment is widely mistaken, that we are influenced by factors that we are ignorant of and would deny as playing a role. It is part of our self-image that these factors not be influential. What this means is that the individual is less the locus of judgment than we assume. I also review studies of moral perception that present us with situations that occasion different moral reactions to situations for which we would have difficulty articulating moral differences. This set of studies challenges our belief in the potential for systematic organization of some high-order principles that can be applied in individual cases. Over the course of the argument, I have to clarify the relevance of the descriptive studies for the normative theories. To this end, I argue that an appreciation of our cognitive and social practices and limits provides us with an understanding of the point of moral life that is both straightforward and compelling. Whereas this chapter is devoted to canvassing data, the next is devoted to interpreting the significance of the data for philosophizing about moral life.

Becoming clearer about moral psychology, we can gain insight into the role of culture and conforming tendencies and pressures in the organization of moral life. Armed with these insights, we can be better situated to offer a realistic interpretation of social freedom and the role privacy plays in structuring this freedom, the goal I set for myself in Chapter 6.

THE NEED TO INTEGRATE ETHICS AND PSYCHOLOGY

Ethics as a philosophical discipline investigates the human good. Characterizations of the human good must depend on a view of human nature, including assessments of human motivational, emotional, judgmental, and cognitive abilities and limitations.

The relationship between what we expect of the reasonable person, the person who gets passing moral grades, and what we find in the normal person is complex and inherently controversial. We could have a situation in which no one acts reasonably. Nevertheless, the reasonable person is not the perfectly reasoning and ideally motivated being, but is the creature with the recognizable cognitive and emotional contours of a human.[1] If we come to think that we have radically misjudged a normal person's abilities, we would be situated to challenge the standard view of how a reasonable person would act, or at least what we regard as reasonable to expect of a person. Minimally, our account of moral thinking should not rest on false portrayals of factors that influence motivation, perception, or judgment.

SOCIAL DIMENSIONS OF ORDINARY PERCEPTION

Some of the most interesting work in social psychology focuses on the contextual influences on judgment in general and on moral judgment in particular. Repeated studies have uncovered something called 'anchoring'.[2] When people are asked to estimate something, such as the speed of a car, the range of the answers suggested by the questioner or other subjects has a gravitational effect on others responding. By offering alternatives with high values, the experimenter can typically influence people to respond with high estimates. The same is true for low estimates.[3]

An early study demonstrating the social influence on individual perception of gravitational effects involved a curious effect of a small light in an otherwise dark room. A stationary point of light in a dark room seems to move back and forth, with different observers reporting different ranges of motion. When several observers are situated together to estimate the range of the apparent motion of the light, the variance in estimates diminishes markedly.[4] The anchoring effect disappears when subjects are told that the light's ostensible motion was illusory and are asked to estimate the apparent motion.[5]

Solomon Asch tested people for their proclivity to conform to erroneous public judgment on a matter that by themselves they would always get correct.[6] People merely had to say which of three lines was closest in length to a given line. No one errs in making this judgment *except* when the person making the comparison knows that all of the other people who were asked the same question concurred in giving a different answer. Specifically, Asch found these results:

> All (or nearly all) subjects reacted with signs of tension and confusion. Roughly one-third of the judgments subjects made were in error. Nearly 80 percent of the subjects gave the obviously wrong answer on at least one trial. The perception that a few other people made an absurd judgment of a clear, unambiguous physical matter was a very troubling experience, sufficient to cause doubt, and in some cases conformity.[7]

As so far described, the Asch experiment leaves unanswered the question of whether the subjects who conformed with an erroneous majority actually came to believe what they reported. Asch tested for this and found that when subjects reported privately rather than publicly, the error rate fell from 33 percent to 7.4 percent.[8] This suggests that most of the errors reported stemmed not from distorted assessments but from pressure to appear like others.[9]

SOCIAL DIMENSIONS OF SOCIAL AND MORAL JUDGMENT

Another experiment, one that severely tests the acceptability of reliance on authority, was conducted by Stanley Milgram.[10] Experimenters assigned subjects the role of asking questions to a person and administering, they believed, increasingly strong shocks when the respondent incorrectly answered questions. The respondent told the subjects that he had a heart condition, and that the shocks could kill him. Nearly all of those who administered the full battery of shocks felt anxiety about their compliance, but when they indicated that they wanted to quit, they were told by the experimenter that they had to continue, that it was in the interest of science that they continue, and finally that the experimenter would take full responsibility if something terrible happened to the respondent. Under some testing conditions, *two-thirds* of those participating continued with the full battery of shocks despite believing that the respondent was being seriously hurt by the shocks and despite wanting to stop the experiment.

Milgram and others described the experimental setup to people and asked them whether they personally would have complied with the experimental protocol and what percentage of real subjects would comply. Nearly all people judged that they personally would not comply and that nearly no one else would either. This disparity between expectation and outcome suggests how little attuned people are to the factors that shape their own judgment and contribute to their own behavior.

Findings that people fail to assess accurately what factors condition our conduct are not unique to Milgram's experimental setup. Nisbett and Wilson argue that actors typically have limited access to their own cognitive processes, and, as a result, they misjudge which causal factors steer their behavior.[11] A study by Latané and Darley showed that in a wide variety of settings, people's willingness to come to the aid of someone in distress varies inversely with the number of other bystanders.[12] Despite their consistent findings about how numbers influence conduct, subjects claimed that it had no effect on them, and that it would not be a factor for others. This denial even survived being apprised of the results of experiments.

Hornstein and others report that they left wallets with a small amount of cash ($2) and personal papers, including a check and identification cards, in midtown Manhattan. They found that 51 percent of these were returned to the ostensible owner, almost 90 percent of these without anything missing. In a variation on this theme, the experimenters left wallets around, but this time with letters attached, indicating that someone tried to return the wallet to the owner. The accompanying letters were either neutral, positive, or negative in tone. In this situation 18 percent of wallets with negative letters were returned, 51 percent of wallets with neutral letters were returned, and 60 percent of wallets with positive letters were returned.[13]

Finally, one can cite the Zimbardo study of subjects role-playing as guards and prisoners.[14] Despite knowing that experimenters assigned them randomly to the position of guard, and that those role-playing as prisoners were fellow experimental subjects just like themselves, brutality soon emerged in the attitudes many "guards" displayed toward the "prisoners." Here the harrowing role-engendered scripts obscured the broader understanding accessible to each subject. Zimbardo describes the value of his study in the following terms:

> The potential social value of this study derives precisely from the fact that normal, healthy, educated young men could be so radically transformed under the institutional pressures of a "prison environment."
>
> The pathology observed in this study cannot be reasonably attributed to pre-existing personality differences of the subjects, that option being eliminated by our selection procedures and random assignment. Rather, the subjects' abnormal social and personal reactions are best seen as a product of their transaction with an environment that supported the behavior that would be pathological in other settings, but was "appropriate" in this prison. Had we observed comparable reactions in a real prison, the psychiatrist undoubtedly would have been able to attribute any prisoner's behavior to character defects or personality maladjustment, while critics of the prison system would have been quick to label the guards as "psychopathic." This tendency to locate the source of behavior disorders inside a particular person or group underestimates the power of situational forces.[15]

We cannot avoid concluding from these studies that our picture of human motivation is radically different from what these studies suggest. We are much more subject to social forces than we suspect, and we are much less adept at countering environmental and social influences and expectations than naïve estimations would have anticipated. People are less the locus of decision and evaluation than we thought. Context and culture loom larger than our common sense estimates would allow.

As the studies in this section indicate, there is compelling evidence that people account for behavior, whether their own or that of others, on the basis of culture-specific causal schemes. That is to say, we have a picture of what makes people behave, and when they behave we attribute factors we think relevant. Because of our understanding of the individual's relationship to her culture and environment, we are likely to attribute nearly all the causal factors to the individual. We are unlikely to attribute environmental factors that have causal relevance. We have seen that these schemes are often inaccurate, resulting in wrongly attributing behavior to less relevant or irrelevant factors.[16] Being unaware of significant causal factors, especially when combined with confidence that one is uninfluenced by them, makes an individual less autonomous than would otherwise be the case. It also makes us poorer predictors and moral evaluators of other people's conduct, because our depiction of the relevant behavioral context is corrupted.

When we judge behavior, we typically have in mind some picture of how we and others would in fact behave in the context. What is the significance of being radically wrong about such base-rate judgments? Does not such conflict between actual and expected behavior suggest that the picture of humankind underlying our moral outlook is wrong in a fundamental way? Should errors of this sort have an effect on our assessment of individual wrongdoers? Should information of the sort that Milgram discovered affect our beliefs about what the "reasonable person" would do in this context, or our degree of censure for someone who complies?[17]

We can differentiate two moral changes that the evidence might occasion. It might affect what we regard as correct behavior; alternatively, it might affect what we deem reasonable to expect of people. All I care to suggest is that we reconsider what it is reasonable to expect of people as we learn more about what factors shape judgment and behavior. That is to say, we need not feel that the Milgram experiment demonstrates that it is right or all right to kill experimental subjects to satisfy scientific curiosity. We don't have to waffle on its wrongness. What we have to consider is whether there is fault, a concept connected with what it is reasonable to expect. Strategies in judgment, like certain levels of precautions against danger to others, are to be judged in large measure by their overall utility.[18] This means that some of what happens that is wrong and regrettable may be properly regarded as done without fault, because there is no feasible alternative.

Thus far we have reviewed some studies that challenge our beliefs about the effects of social and environmental influences on individual moral judgment. There is interesting recent work on moral perception that is worth reviewing. It suggests that rather than applying a given and fixed set of moral principles to particular situations as they arise, the situation largely evokes the principles that are applied. As we will see, the same objective state can invoke different sets of principles, depending on how the state is represented.

Kahneman, Knetsch, and Thaler show that the framing effects occur in perceptions of fairness. Wage adjustments coded as losses are regarded as unfair, though the same adjustments are regarded as fair when coded as a gain. In situation A, a company finding itself in the midst of substantial unemployment and no inflation, decides to cut wages by 7 percent. Of their sample, 62 percent found this move *unfair*. In situation B, where there is substantial unemployment and 12 percent inflation, the company raises wages only 5 percent. Of their sample, 78 percent found this *fair*. In both situations, workers end up with 7 percent less real wages.

Miller and McFarland conducted a study to test norm theory.[19] According to norm theory, we judge some state of affairs as normal on the basis of the difficulty with which we can imagine alternatives, rather than on the basis of its dominating probability. If an event occurs and we can readily imagine alternatives, the event will seem abnormal. Alternatively, if we have difficulty imagining alternatives, the event will seem normal. For instance, consider two people who are greatly delayed by a flight. Suppose one person just switched at the last minute to the particular flight, whereas the other was scheduled for weeks to be on the flight. From a strictly statistical perspective, there is no greater probability that the flight switched to was more likely to be delayed than the flight originally scheduled. Still, the person who switched flights will feel more regret than the other person because the alternative of staying on the originally scheduled flight seems so "available" in the case of the person who switched.[20]

Furthermore, the more an event evokes alternatives, the stronger the emotional reactions to the event will be. This has an impact on which actions of ours we find regrettable. For instance, we will feel more regret if we are in an accident on our way home from work if we have taken an alternative route than if we are in an accident using our normal route.[21]

Miller and McFarland studied attitudes about victim compensation for people attacked while shopping at a grocery store. There were two different scenarios for the attack. In one scenario, the victim was shopping at his usual store. In the second, he was shopping at a store that he rarely frequented. Miller and McFarland found: "Subjects assigned the victim who was shot at a store he rarely visited significantly more compensation than the victim who was shot at his regular store."[22] Subjects recommended over $100,000 more for the same injury in the exceptional context than they did in the routine context![23] Apparently, subjects felt it to be more unfair to be shot at a store one rarely frequented than at one commonly frequented.

In a related branch of studies, people were found to raise or lower their estimation of a person's responsibility for an event on the basis of whether there was a way of compensating or rectifying *after the fact of the event*. The driving mechanism here is a belief in the world as a just system. We adjust our attributions to maintain this outlook. This comes out dramatically in a study on attributions of people who have been raped. Although people would punish a rapist more for raping a virgin than a divorcée, these same people would find more fault with the virgin than with the divorcée for the rape. Ironically, because there is perceived to be a greater violation in the case of the rape of the virgin than in the rape of a divorcée, a harsher judgment of the virgin is necessary to explain her suffering if the world is to be seen as just.[24]

Should we write off all the tendencies just cited as evidence of a moral illusion because we cannot articulate their moral grounding? Our answer to this will depend on our confidence in our capacity to model good judgment explicitly. Bayesian decision making has been criticized on the grounds that it is not clear that we would in fact make more rational or better decisions if we confined our considerations to the factors that we could represent on decision trees. Similar questions can be raised about the principle of articulate rationality. If we restrict our judgments to those that we could rationally defend or defend in light of moral theory, how well would we track behavior we regard as sensible and reasonable? But modulating our acceptance of articulate rationality means that at times at least we are willing to abide by standards of judgment whose superiority over other standards cannot be established. In the next chapter, I discuss alternative approaches to gutting our normal responses when these fail to accord with dominant moral theories.

Someone might observe that my claim about the degree of influence of culture on moral judgment is not something that would surprise Mill and the others I discussed – indeed their whole concern is with counteracting the pervasiveness of such influence in part by making it visible and showing that there are rational and autonomy-promoting alternatives. These studies show how people ordinarily judge, not how they either must or should judge.

Furthermore, Mill and other theorists I have criticized can claim that there is an alternative to situation-determined norms of application, if that is thought desirable. That alternative is explicit use of the theories in all these cases and simply ignoring disparities occasioned by framing effects and other sorts of "distortions." Those theorists who seek "reflective equilibrium" between their theories and intuitive reactions may feel more challenged by the data.

SOME WORRIES

Criticism of the potential moral relevance of the studies described in this chapter might follow several lines of attack. First, one might be suspicious of the representativeness of the population tested in the studies cited. A large percentage of studies are conducted on middle-class psychology students in their introductory course in psychology. Second, one might worry that the people on whom the tests are conducted are first-world, middle-class people. How can this teach us about human nature in general? Indeed, if the thesis that people are largely subject to cultural influences is correct, then it follows from these very studies that people in diverse cultures would react differently. So again, how can we get universal information about human nature from these studies? Third, these studies do not take account of how human nature is historical. Discoveries of our nature enable us to transform, potentially falsify, the nature revealed.

Several responses can be offered here. The main lesson I have claimed we learn is the extent of our cultural susceptibility. *This claim* is not undermined by the prospect that in different cultures, people would act differently. People can behave differently from culture to culture without the susceptibility of their behavior to culture being different. But then one can raise the question whether susceptibility to culture differs from culture to culture. Here again I believe we cannot answer this question affirmatively without conceding the cultural dimension to the issue.

Does my claim about our cultural susceptibility then become a necessary truth for which empirical evidence is not necessary? If the evidence, however it comes out, supports a thesis, then it seems as if evidence is irrelevant to the thesis.

Might it not be true after all that people in different cultures are differentially susceptible to cultural influence without this showing the inevitability of just one level of cultural dependency? Might there not be cultural reasons why people just are less vulnerable to cultural norms? In the next two chapters, I argue that being culturally less vulnerable means something different from what we associate with the prospect. I argue that there are in fact different levels of cultural dependence, but that for most people, this difference is a difference in variety of directions of susceptibility rather than in the overall level of susceptibility. The difference is significant, but its analysis is quite unlike that which is presupposed in standard discussions.

The importance of considering these experiments lies in realizing the potential impact empirical findings can have on our understanding the nature of morality as well as the scope and limits of social norms.[25]

CONCLUSION

We seem highly disposed to judge not by reference to a decontextualized yardstick against which we measure the world, but rather by reference to what we find our situation to be. We are in motion, as Copernicus taught us, and our assessments of the world, moral and factual, reflect this instability, this sensitivity to changing contexts. Evaluation is not a process that engages all of our potentially relevant principles and rules with a situation, but only the resultant of those values evoked. The patterns that determine whether a given norm will be evoked are complex and highly culturally contingent.

Few moral philosophers would follow Kant in arguing that empirical aspects of human nature are morally irrelevant. Despite this distancing from the extreme indifference to empirical dimensions of the self, moral and social philosophers have been by and large oblivious to empirical discoveries about human nature and judgment. There is enough that is mistaken or questionable about our view of how people work to encourage rethinking our moral outlook in light of available data. In the next chapter I try to draw some lessons from the discussion in this chapter about the domain of morality and the role culture and conformity play within morality. This revised view of culture and conformity within morality opens the way to a new interpretation of social freedom and privacy.

Chapter 5

The importance of cultural authority for morality

> A cultureless human being would probably turn out to be not an intrinsically talented though unfulfilled ape, but a wholly mindless and consequently unworkable monstrosity. Like the cabbage it so much resembles, the *Homo sapiens* brain, having arisen within the framework of human culture, would not be viable outside of it. (Clifford Geertz, *Interpretations of Culture*)

In Chapter 4, our focus was on disparities between moral judgmental practice and widespread beliefs about what influences moral judgment. The burden of this chapter is to suggest the relevance of some of these findings to our conception of morality. In emphasizing conforming tendencies as corrective and salutary, as I do in this chapter, I do not mean to be seen as arguing that either cultures generally or those around one in particular are all one needs for a morally informed life. Rather, I want to highlight the morally constructive dimensions of socialization and conforming tendencies. In so doing, I hope to counteract the tendency in philosophy to regard these tendencies as slavish and corrupting. Conformity uncompromised *is* mindless. But autonomy uncompromised is sociopathic.

What makes autonomy uncompromised sociopathic is its refusal to accept any authority but that of the agent's own judgment. We saw that much of moral philosophy applauds the effort to undermine the authority of culture, traditions, associations, and institutions, relegating to the individual the role of validating whatever is to be accepted, without primary or basic reliance on any of these sources. The prospect that this makes sense as an interpretation of morality is challenged in this chapter.

If my claims are right, then morality and culture are much more intimately bound than many philosophers recognize, and the social forces that maintain cultural and associational ties intact will be seen as playing important moral roles. Privacy and social pressure will emerge as two critical factors in maintaining human ties in a way that generates prospects for social freedom.

INTERPRETING THE STUDIES:
A CONSTRUCTIVE OUTLOOK ON CONFORMITY

Chapter 3 documents how philosophers are especially prone to think that judgment should be individually, rationally, and aculturally validated in order to display the full features of critical, moral understanding. In accord with this accepted outlook of moral theory, the standard conclusion that people draw from experiments like the Milgram, Asch, Zimbardo, and Sherif studies, reviewed in Chapter 4, is that people should learn how to rely on their own judgment in the face of discomforting, social disagreement.[1] Notice though that regarding oneself as an authority on moral matters, particularly controversial ones, would be treated as pitifully arrogant in any other field of judgment. It is comparable with people's confidently denying the adequacy of Bell's Inequality or the Banach-Tarski Theorem because the experiments or proofs made no sense to them.[2]

Alternatively, one might discover in these results a tendency to count on the corrective influence of others when one's own assessment garners no independent support. Focusing again on some of these experiments might help us see them in a different light, one in which individuals sensibly recognize their own limitations and count on others to help eliminate error. Recall the study that showed the anchoring effect in the context of a still light that appeared to move. The anchoring effect dissipated when subjects were told the motion was apparent. Or consider the Asch experiment in which people felt pressured by others' assessments of the length of a line. In real life we think it stubborn and irrational, not principled, for people to insist that they are right about an observation and all others wrong when the others are situated just as well to judge. Or take the Zimbardo experiment, finding guards and prisoners overly ready to adopt the patterns implicit in their assigned roles. In general, though not in every instance, it is appropriate for individuals to adopt the persona of a role when they are cast in that role. We think a judge, for instance, has a duty to decide a case in light of relevant legal principles, not on the basis of a preferred personal moral theory.[3] In general, this role-conforming attitude makes sense as a strategy. It reveals something important about our moral nature missed by interpretations of morality that place a high premium on articulate rationality.

Solomon Asch, whose studies we reviewed in Chapter 4, interprets the shift of individuals' assessments toward authoritative or peer assessment as a critical piece of social dynamics. Asch points out that psychologists see the phenomenon of conformity as either the result of an effort to avoid social punishment or achieve social rewards on the one hand, or as the effect of manipulation by those with power or authority on those without these qualities on the other hand. Both of these perspectives presuppose that the shift occurs in only one direction. Asch questions this presupposition, suggests that the shifts are bidirectional, and proposes that we see the phenomenon as a group process that has the character of a group achievement. We can judge the conforming phenomenon not as a distortion of individual rationality but as an essential factor in promoting social being.[4] Unless we were strongly susceptible to the practices of those around us, we would never develop as social beings, and we could not participate in a common life. This is a simple point ignored by the theories insistent on use of the principle of articulate rationality.

Learning takes place via trust in certain formal and informal authorities: parents, teachers, community leaders, elected officials, religious leaders, and the common behavior patterns one sees around oneself. In the law of torts, customary practice provides presumptive evidence as to the reasonableness of conduct.[5] These paradigms of social learning, belonging, and participation, and thereby of moral being, are genetically, epistemologically, and practically indispensable to moral judgment. Our cognitive and moral economies require that we rely on such authorities for the bulk of our everyday judgments.[6]

There is something morally illuminating to be found in our cultural susceptibilities and character. Throughout human existence, communities have developed stylized artifacts and behavior, these stylizations reflecting a level of concern not captured in a focus on the achievement of any external objective. The primary objective of these concerns is group identity and cultural sharing. The remnants of the earliest known communities illustrate these ubiquitous elaborations adorning all things human.[7] Parents encourage behavior patterns in their children that assure participation in the community, and not just the nonsocial ends that are achievable through group effort and coordination. Parents raise their children to be civilized and culturally embedded.[8] This suggests the necessity of an extension of the rationales for conduct and institutions that moral theorists have been willing to endorse. It suggests that participating in a culture is an end in itself, aside from the other goods it promotes. In contrast to this suggestion, modern moral theories characteristically treat cultural participation as instrumental at best.[9]

By seeing morality as grounded in culture, we locate its goal in the goal of culture, that being a life in community with others. Grounding value on sharing community and culture with others is simpler, inherently more appealing, and more direct than grounding value in some of the standard moral rationales, including coordination strategies, self-interest, being able to justify ourselves to others, according others equal concern and respect, or acting on the basis of pure practical reason.[10] If participating in one's community is valuable and fundamental, then morality is to be seen as a major aspect

69

of this participation. We then see some of the cognitive practices described in Chapter 4, practices that emphasize our dependence on the outlook of others for our bearings and directions, as being directly conducive to the end of participation in community life.

Annette Baier's treatment of trust fashions a more plausible foundation for moral life than do many of the theoretical constructions current in our literature. Baier shows that we do not even get to step one in any moral construction unless we presuppose trust between people who are inherently dependent and vulnerable. Among the aspects of trust that fit the picture I am proposing is that aspect that relates to caring about a common good. According to Baier,

> The best reason for confidence in another's good care of what one cares about is that it is a common good, and the best reason for thinking that one's own good is a common good is being loved. This may not, usually will not, ensure agreement on what best should be done to take care of that good, but it rules out suspicion of ill will.[11]

Our social nature, our tendency to internalize what we see around us, ensures that there is some common good, some ends, or interrelated set of ends, we all wish to see realized through our group endeavors. We not only take aim at ends together; we aim to work together in bringing them about. The latter process being as important as the former, the prospect of social solidarity is central to our way of being. Two features are to be emphasized: the common ends and our agency as cooperating social beings.

It is misleading to think of pursuit of common ends as egoistic on the grounds that common ends are, after all, ends individuals *happen to* share. What this thought leaves out of account is that the reason individuals adopt common ends is that they are common, and immersion in these provides a way of being social.

There is a central lesson in this discussion. Our tendency to be part of a social group, our inclination to share life and see the world as others around us see it, our dependence on cultural bonds with others for a meaningful life – these are deep features of the human experience. They directly reflect cultural and biological needs and dependencies. These needs and dependencies, our experience as cultural beings, are obscured by and incompatible with moral reconstructions and interpretations that focus on articulate rationality and the autonomous features of judgment it highlights. On the standard moral constructions, our cultural and group tendencies are antithetical to moral experience. On the alternative, they are central to it, and should have a prominent role in moral understanding.

AN EVOLUTIONARY PERSPECTIVE ON MORALITY, RATIONALITY, AND THE AUTHORITY OF CULTURE

In a speculative essay on social evolution,[12] Donald Campbell suggests that a universal tendency to conform to the opinions of others, especially prestige figures, may be an essential, socially adaptive mechanism, and not the character defect typically discovered in these conforming practices. Campbell points out that for this mechanism to succeed in retaining adaptive social customs, it would have to "operate blindly, without regard to apparent functionality."

Along similar lines, Allan Gibbard provides an evolutionary account of human sensitivity to social rules and practices.[13] Gibbard finds in susceptibility to social surroundings evidence that coordination with others is an adaptive mechanism critical to our success as a species. Susceptibility to cultural pressures at times competes, not always unfavorably, with tendencies toward systematic rationality, like the search for consistency in standards and for axiomatic structure. (I will offer evidence that the human drive to consistency in standards is less pressing than philosophers, including Gibbard, assume.)

In Gibbard's account, the tendency to social accommodation is explained, but not typically motivated, by natural selection. Individuals do not seek to coordinate in order to promote the proliferation of their genetic code. Rather, because coordinating strategies have been helpful to the survival of genes that dispose their hosts in that way, caring how others view one becomes an important motivator in human psychology.

Thus far the evolutionary talk has been speculative and at least at some level consistent with many of the standard theoretic approaches to moral being. I wish now to extend the discussion of evolution and moral–social being by correcting a perspective common among moral theorists. As we saw in the preceding chapter, moral and social character is sometimes explained as an adaptation that helps fundamentally selfish or asocial beings solve "prisoner's dilemma" sorts of problems.[14] Social character, it is suggested, is the best strategy for serving selfish ends. This strategy is most explicit in the contract tradition. The presupposition of this outlook, and it is one found in the work of some of the most eminent social theorists, is that the human organic character is completed *before* social strategies emerge. There is reason, however, to think otherwise – that our social and cultural characteristics and our brains evolved simultaneously. This suggests that the type of character that much moral theory is meant to address and appeal to is very different than the sort we find ourselves to be. Clifford Geertz has elegantly argued for this picture of the fundamental social character of the mind in several essays.

> Recent research in anthropology suggests that the prevailing view that the mental dispositions of man are genetically prior to culture and that his actual capabilities represent the amplification or extension of these pre-existent dispositions by cultural means is incorrect. The apparent fact that the final stages of the biological evolution of man occurred after the initial stages of the growth of culture implies that "basic," "pure," or "unconditioned," human nature, in the sense of the innate constitution of man, is so functionally incomplete as to be unworkable. Tools, hunting, family organization, and, later, art, religion, and "science" molded man somatically; and they are, therefore, necessary not merely to his survival but to his existential realization.[15]

In another essay,[16] Geertz argues that cultural adaptation is not a means to extending the mental functions we possess but a precondition of having these functions in the first place:

> The Pleistocene period, with its rapid and radical variations in climate, land formations, and vegetation, has long been recognized to be a period in which conditions were ideal for the speedy and efficient evolutionary development of man; now it seems also to have been a period in which a cultural environment increasingly supplemented the natural environment in the selection process so as to further accelerate the rate of hominid evolution to an unprecedented speed. The Ice Age appears not to have been merely a time of receding brow ridges and shrinking jaws, but a time in which were forged nearly all those characteristics of man's existence which are most graphically human: his thoroughly encephelated nervous system, his incest-taboo-based social structure, and his capacity to create and use symbols. The fact that these distinctive features of humanity emerged together in complex interaction with one another rather than serially as for so long supposed is of exceptional importance in the interpretation of human mentality, because it suggests that man's nervous system does not merely enable him to acquire culture, it positively demands that he do so if it is going to function at all. Rather than culture acting only to supplement, develop, and extend organically based capacities logically and genetically prior to it, it would seem to be ingredient to those capacities themselves. A cultureless human being would probably turn out to be not an intrinsically talented though unfulfilled ape, but a wholly mindless and consequently unworkable monstrosity.[17]

> The human nervous system relies, inescapably, on the accessibility of public symbolic structures to build up its own autonomous, ongoing pattern of activity.[18]

This account of the human relationship to culture and life with others suggests that the way methodological and foundational issues are addressed in moral and social philosophy is misguided. The fact that technical elegance abounds is not enough to make the approach illuminating or scientific if the way the fundamental problems are framed is based on a specious picture of a person's relationship to others.

What we have been suggesting is that human rationality is best understood as a socially infused and validated process, not a Cartesian enterprise. Furthermore, this social dimension is not a strategy for advancing individually given ends but is intrinsic to the ends sought and even the capacity to seek ends.

Adopting this perspective on rationality and social process does not preclude individuals from using the tools of the social process to articulate or challenge the process. It only precludes the prospect of counting on rationality to eliminate or replace culture as the core and source of our human capacities.

AUTHORITY AND INDIVIDUAL JUDGMENT

In Chapters 2 and 3, I detailed the suspicion toward culture that runs rampant among moral theorists. Being suspicious of the corrupting, polluting influence of local culture, philosophers have sought an Archimedean point, whether rationally or empirically grounded, that will provide a route to rational and moral reflection that is independent of cultural influences. I pointed out that to pass the test of being culturally uncorrupted, the notion of rational validation had to be interpreted in terms that enabled individual application.

In the portrayals of moral philosophy we considered, there was a common assumption about the *sorts* of reasons that can be used in moral or philosophical analysis. The assumption is that for an individual to have a deep moral understanding, she must be able to supply reasons for her moral practices and beliefs that make no reference to the practices or opinions of others. We are now able to bring more resolution to our understanding of what is problematical about discounting culture in theoretical constructions of moral life.

In discussing the nature of authority, Joseph Raz has differentiated first-order from second-order reasons. A first-order reason is a reason that speaks directly to the merits of a case. A second-order reason, in contrast, is a reason for disregarding at least some first-order reasons. If there are second-order reasons, there are reasons that blind us practically to the influence of some relevant considerations. Examples of excluding reasons are traffic lights and parental orders. Each of these precludes the people subject to the rule from acting on certain reasons for acting, such as no other traffic coming or a strong desire not to clean one's room. Conceptually, authority depends for its possibility on there being second-order reasons, blinding influences, that preclude us from legitimately acting on the merits of a case directly.

[R. P. Wolff] sees correctly that legitimate authority involves a denial of one's right to act on the merits of the case. But the reformulation also shows where he went wrong. He tacitly and correctly assumes that reason never justifies abandoning one's autonomy, that is, one's right and duty to act on one's judgment of what ought to be done, *all things considered.* I shall call this the principle of autonomy. He also tacitly and wrongly assumes that this is identical with the false principle that there are not valid exclusionary reasons, that is, that one is never justified in not doing what ought to be done on the balance of first-order reasons. I shall call this the denial of authority.

This confusion is natural if one conceives of all reasons as essentially first-order reasons and overlooks the possibility of the existence of second-order reasons. If all valid reasons are first-order reasons then it is a necessary truth that the principle of autonomy entails the denial of authority, for then what ought to be done all things considered is identical with what ought to be done on the balance of first-order reasons. But since there could in principle be valid second-order reasons, there is nothing in the principle of autonomy that requires the rejection of all authority.[19]

Characteristic of moral theory's treatment of culture and tradition generally is to treat them as suspect until proven on the basis of a narrow range of considerations: hence the states of nature and the veils of ignorance. This approach is not neutral between starting points. It guarantees that certain sorts of considerations are systematically excluded – considerations that rely on our realizations of our own individual limitations and our appreciation of factors we cannot fully appreciate or articulate as individuals at a given time. It commits us to conceptually dumping authorities and structures that we might trust to have more value than *we* can establish.

At first glance, it would seem as if all reasoning has to be *grounded* in first-order reasons for it to be a reason at all. Either there is a first-order reason for doing something, or there is a second-order reason that is grounded in first-order reasons for disregarding first-order reasons directly. This outlook would vindicate the standard approach I am criticizing: Only trust authorities that are first-order defensible.

It begs the question to suppose that we do not need to rely on authority, particularly on the authority of one's culture, to know how to establish the relevance of first-order reason. We place enormous confidence in our reasoning skills and information base to trust them rather than what we see around us when those surroundings have served us rather well. Even something as straightforward as mathematical and logical reasoning is not immune from needing cultural validation. I can grasp what a truth table is, and I can understand a definition of validity. But I know that I and others have been persuaded that forms of reasoning are impeccable only later to discover hidden assumptions or subtle confusions. I also know that there are various paradoxes concerning the foundations of these domains of thought, paradoxes I would not have discovered on my own, and whose significance I cannot estimate. Consequently I realize that my own judgment about adequacy is of limited value. What choice have I but to defer to others and rely on methods others recommend, independent of what my own first-order reasoning would suggest? (Think of the square root of -1.)

The standard of articulate rationality ensures that only first-order reasons are available for resolution of moral issues. Recognition of personal limitations is not representable as a first-order reason. It is a higher-order reason giving one reason to discount one's own reason. But even some who reject the principle of articulate rationality would argue that authority to be justified must be justified in terms of good reasons that are applicable independent of the authoritative order or regime.[20] This concept too is a mistake, for reasons parallel to those just cited. We need to rely on authorities to establish the claim that something is a good reason, first or higher order.

Clearly people regard culture as playing an authoritative role in their lives, and the analysis in terms of independent good reasons seems oblivious to this.[21] If culture and tradition are sources of practical insight, we need to explore how this is. Two possibilities surface as closest to standard outlooks presented in the moral literature. First, culture is the repository of vindicated perspectives, perspectives that in principle can be discerned right independently. It is relatively uncontroversial to think that culture is authoritative in this way.

A second view of the authority of culture involves saliently resolving matters that require strategies – for instance, enforcing solutions for prisoner's dilemma problems and determining how coordination problems are to be addressed. The specific cultural mode is not independently valid. There is a need to have some mode, and given that others are banking on this system, it becomes right for others to comply with it as well.[22] On this view, culture has authority because it indicates which method of coordination is the adopted one. Here too culture can seem uncontroversially authoritative.

Cultures have authority for the reasons suggested, but these reasons do not exhaust the ways cultures are authoritative for people. What is missing is the extent to which an individual finds that elements of her own nature are "out there" in the culture or tradition to be discovered. In the way that by learning about our families we learn about ourselves, by learning about our cultures we appreciate dimensions of ourselves otherwise inaccessible. In this process we learn more than facts about ancestors or childhood influences. We also learn something about what we are implicitly and what directions our future might meaningfully take.

Also what is missing is a way of living life with others whose value is not explained by being a repository for tested ways of doing things or by concern for coordination and efficiency. Despite knowing that there are many cultural forms in which people relate adequately, we find embedded in ourselves ways of relating that we discover fulfillment in maintaining. Despite being one of many, we can take pride in its perspective and display confidence in its workings. We are interpersonally oriented. We find value in this and treat it as something to be sustained through self-conscious identification and education. Very clearly people find it important to preserve their own culture and take responsibility for this. This is so despite the absence of proof or arguments that one culture is better than another or that one would have been better off in this culture than in an alternative culture.

Culture is only one of multiple sources of self-discovery, direction, and fulfillment, but it is experienced as having weight for decisions. As such it is authoritative. There are limited but varied enforcement mechanisms that confront someone who attempts to opt out of any particular cultural structure. Some effective informal enforcement mechanisms will be discussed in the next chapter. Like other putative authorities, culture is not beyond criticism or challenge. Like other authorities, it does not have to establish its own credentials at every juncture, and it is capable of excluding certain types of first-order reasons from having practical effect.

In claiming that culture has authority, one is not committing to claiming that it has more weight than all other considerations, whether taken singly or combined. If harm is done through doing things this way, and the harm can be averted through alternatives that are relatively costless, then the authority of cultural ways has little weight. Not only will cultures normally have room for maneuvering to avert harms in these situations, but typically cultures will represent a variety of perspectives, from which those considering an approach can choose. There may be little or no harm in the cultural restriction and some benefit in sustaining the cultural mode. Then the claim is entitled to considerable weight. Why groups, like cultures, are entitled to authority will be further developed in the next chapter.

Is the authority of culture secondary, in the sense that its justification or legitimacy is based on its role in helping people act on reasons that *independently* bind or weigh on them, as Joseph Raz argues?[23] I think the answer to this question is no. That cultures help people fulfill basic obligations is not in dispute. But whether their value derives solely from this is questionable, as I have been arguing. To think that cultures can be disqualified from having authority because of the way they botch important functions is very far from thinking that cultures or everything authoritative earn authority in virtue of promoting proper practices. A person may be disqualified from holding national office because he has repeatedly molested children; yet not molesting children is neither justification nor qualification, let alone authority, for holding office.

Why might not associations of people derive authority from the good they can do independent of whether they result in making people more effective duty compliers or more effective at controlling their actions? After all, Raz recognizes authorities, inspirational authorities, whose title to authority and whose influence on others has little to do with encouragement to dutiful behavior or action on the basis of reason.[24]

SOME OBJECTIONS CONSIDERED

Four questions to my interpretation of morality will be raised, and in addressing these, some of the alleged virtues of moral theory seen as culturally independent will be critically examined: (1) Without theory, how is criticism possible? (2) How are moral conflicts to be resolved without theory? (3) Don't theories introduce culturally and historically unprecedented ideas? (4) Doesn't the human drive for consistency and coherence across the various social and personal domains have a long-term tendency to result in social rules that are culturally nonspecific and thus universal in scope?

A central objection: How is criticism possible?

Philosophers, as I have illustrated, often adopt the position that social and moral criticism would not be possible unless one had access to a culturally independent perspective. We do not require some socially and culturally independent theory to account for changes, even moral changes, within our practices. Changes can occur because of the inner dynamics of practice, shifting environmental variables, and cross-cultural influences rather than from theoretically driven efforts. Thus, concerns critical of cultural forms arising within cultures do not presuppose a culturally autonomous perspective. Various factors can drive reflection and criticism within a cultural setting.

There is a tendency to regard acting on social norms as acting like an automaton.[25] Yet, social norms rarely require or permit such rigidity. Invariably, there are unresolved competing and inconsistent internal objectives that generate movement from within the norm-constituted practices. These (among other) factors make interpretation of norms and contexts necessary, and the evolution of norms possible.[26]

The tendency just mentioned is fueled by a conceptual mistake in inferring that we are unequipped to be reflective about "the culture" because we are socialized in "the culture." Culture in general, and especially our culture, comprises an intricate assortment of associations, many of which compete or overlap in function. This means that what we refer to when we consider "the culture" is not a theoretically homogeneous, hierarchically ordered set of beliefs and principles (or blinders, as some would have it), but rather a bazaar of values and outlooks – microcultures. Each of these microcultures provides a perspective. The diversity of perspectives each person has, just in normal participation in life, is capable of generating interesting and constructive tensions in assessment, without ever escaping "the culture." I show in Chapter 6 how this variety of microcultures is principally responsible for our social freedom.

We can consider and debate issues only once we have a basic, and inevitably culturally loaded, understanding.[27] We can and do argue profitably about how our practices should change.[28] We typically do this without reference to a theory and without aiming at a theory. If one considers some of the central social issues we face, such as how to regard abortion, how to interpret free speech, what type of influence to exercise in Central America, what equality of treatment means in the case of women, we see that what differentiates the best from the most trivial treatments is not the presence or even the prominence of a theory.[29] Indeed, application of a theory is most likely to seem mechanical and forced.

Let me illustrate this last point. Prevalent in recent literature on equality is a call to the elimination of differences in treatment between men and woman, between people of different races, between people of different religions, and between people of different economic standings. Writers of the highest repute place equality in some form at the apex of the political, social, and moral pantheon.[30] But what is meant by equality? Some of those advocating the elimination of differences in treatment focus on formal criteria, like provision of similar educational resources, while others focus on the comparative effective value of opportunities.[31] Before we can know how important equality is, we must know both what is meant by it and what effects it will have on a given community or on a range of communities. This means that we cannot avoid questioning some proposed value as a goal by differentiating at this level between ideals and policies, between theories and their implementation, or between concepts and conceptions.[32] Because of the harm to women's interests and prospects some equal treatment measures caused, as occurred in the aftermath of removing presumptions favoring maternal custody and alimony, there are feminists who advocate abandoning requirements of equal treatment.[33] Recognition of differences in some areas of concern is replacing calls for claims that differences should not be given legal recognition. In some of the feminist literature, this change in ideals advocated is labeled substituting concern for gender disadvantage for the more traditional concern for gender difference.[34]

As we focus more on an intercultural context, especially one that recognizes gender and status differences as central to social organization, depending on what else was true of the society, we might well think they would be ill-advised to regard liberal principles as preferable.[35] Curiously, people tending to liberal values locally based on universal principles also tend to be tolerant of alternatives in other cultures. This tolerance reflects the practical sensitivity to what is theoretically denied: the principle that right cannot be legislated independent of cultural context.

The sorts of criticisms of practices we can meaningfully discuss are those that emerge from considerations *internal to practices*. Inevitably, this makes us vulnerable to most of the judgmental prejudices that our society promotes, just as we are subject to the scientific misconceptions our current theories promote. Progress in change is calculated by demonstrating a local improvement. Such an improvement is measured by the practices that guide the field, rather than by comparing the practices before and after change against some external, theoretically sanctioned, standard of truth to which none of us has access. We do not have perfectly reasons-responsive principles among which to choose. All that is available to us are better and worse strategies for managing particular domains of behavior. But one of the functions that culturally shared strategies do for us is to maintain a life in common.

It might be charged that I have missed *the* central impetus to moral inquiry and to the conception of oneself as a moral being. Isn't there something better than what we find around us, whose very possibility inspires us and demands something of us? I agree that there is, but we should locate the terms and attractiveness of this possibility in the practices themselves and not in higher-order theorizing. There is more to a social practice than just a reflection of what is. There is the culturally implicit direction of the practice that makes demands on it once individuals aim at interpreting it.[36] There is more richness and dimensionality to these practices than philosophers have been able to capture by relegating social practices to the category of *the actual*, to be contrasted with *the ethical*. It is the force of these practice-implicit norms that makes us aware of the category of the ethical as something different. Philosophers have gone astray to the extent that they fail to locate the seeds of this contrast within the cultural norms themselves.

Finally, we can suggest that moral change is better tracked by nontheoretical and culturally embedded processes than by theoretical approaches to moral understanding. As Edna Ullmann-Margalit has shown,[37] we usually cast the distinction between types of norm change in terms of evolution and conscious revision. Attitudes toward norm change differentiate conservatives, who favor evolution as the primary source of change, and enlightenment proponents, who opt for revision according to rational patterns. Ullmann-Margalit suggests that something lies in between these two poles of evolution and revision: norm revision that reflects change rather than imposes it. This third category allows us to appreciate how norms can reflect evolving circumstances and (even enlightened) attitudes without being principally motivated by appeal to an external standard. Ullmann-Margalit points out that norm revision can principally evolve along the lines of reclassifying how unclear cases are handled, leaving resolution of clear cases intact.

Another objection: Only theories resolve moral conflict

An objection one might raise to the analysis offered here argues that majorities, experts, and social practice are all fine so long as they give a clear reading of what we should do. But what about situations where they give conflicting advice? Kant and Mill alike argue that at just this point of conflict common standards must be supplemented with a moral theory that can then resolve the clash. When authorities disagree, how can we adjudicate without appeal to a higher theory?

Of course, one can generate an answer to a controversial moral problem by use of a theory that recognizes less than all the relevant considerations – something moral theories inevitably do – but that does not resolve the problem. It only satisfies the theorist. If conflicting authorities do disagree, it might be because there is a real moral dilemma. What we need here is judgment, not another theory. For instance, if we are considering whether according equal rights for women means according them the same or different rights men are recognized as having, we could, if we chose, employ a utilitarian, a Rawlsian, or a Kantian approach. But once we get the result, we feel no more enlightened or confident than before we applied the preferred theory. We need a great deal of local understanding to discern what is at issue in this context and ones like it. Theories seem inept at supplying what is required. Colleagues specializing in medical ethics have informed me that the earlier practice of addressing issues by the laying out of theoretical perspectives has been discontinued because of the tendency of theoretical approaches to mechanically bulldoze their way through issues.

Don't theories make unique historical contributions that cannot be explained historically?

Philosophers adopt a distorted picture of the contributions of moral theory because they find elements or moves of ordinary thinking that they attribute to great moral theorists. For instance, if people are discussing an issue and somebody asks whether one policy adequately respects the people concerned or whether people are made better off by one policy, philosophers will see this as vindicating Kant's or Mill's moral theory. Really, what it shows is that Kant and Mill appropriated elements of ordinary moral rationality and gave them a dominant role in their philosophy. Sharing these values with Kant or Mill does not mean that the culture derived them from Kant or Mill. What would make the society Kantian would be a *restriction* of considerations to those that can be articulated by using the categorical imperative. What would make it Millian would be a *restriction* of considerations to those of welfare gauged in terms of pleasure. Fortunately, the culture we live in would not tolerate either of these limitations.

Still, it is only fair to concede that theories have historical impact, often promoting ideas that become influential despite being unconventional. It is, however, not only theories that do this. Novels, songs, poems, strikes, protests, slogans, practices – all of these are sources from which ideas emerge into history.

If a moral dilemma can be resolved it will be because judgment, not theory, applied to the problem. What this judgment will have to draw on is an imaginative use of an unlimited range of considerations generally recognized or arguably recognizable as relevant. Bernard Williams, like Charles Stevenson before him, has persuasively argued that theories may do as much to blind us to moral features as to make them salient.[38] He points out that structural features of theorizing may inherently lead to such blinding. Moral theory characteristically looks for considerations that are very general and have as little distinctive content as possible, because it tries to systematize and represent as many reasons as possible as applications of other reasons. In contrast to this, normal critical reflection seeks for as much shared understanding as it can find on any issue and can employ *any* ethical material that makes sense, without first establishing its theoretical pedigree.

Notice that Norm Theory, mentioned in the preceding chapter, fits the Williams–Stevenson view much better than it does approaches to moral thought that offer complete and comprehensive principles. According to Norm Theory, we bring normative categories into play on the basis of salient features of the context, recognizing that what will seem salient will depend on how we initially classify the experience. Norm Theory then studies the factors leading to the variability of which norms are called into operation by an incident. This contrasts with the standard view, according to which we have all the norms available and simply apply *all* those whose antecedent condition is satisfied by the experience.[39]

The innate drive for consistency and coherence

Recent studies speak to the issue of how important it is to people in general to eliminate any normative discrepancies that arise between different sphere-relative norms. For instance, does it strike us as troublesome that we deal with needy strangers within our own country differently than we deal with needy strangers native to other countries? Some would suggest that such discrepancies irritate the human psyche until some conceptual or behavioral surgery alters the profile of these two norms: Either the moral difference becomes articulated or the norm differences continue to seem arbitrary and there is pressure to eliminate them.

Studies of how people deal with cognitive dissonance suggest that dissonance is generated by a threat to one's sense of personal adequacy, and that this can be addressed by a variety of means, just so long as these means reaffirm the value of the threatened self. According to Claude Steele: "Apparently, dissonance can be reduced without altering or adding to the cognitions involved in the provoking inconsistency; it is the image of the self that is at issue, not the inconsistency of cognitions."[40] Steele argues that the evidence cited in the psychological literature that cognitive inconsistency is inherently disturbing confounds the effects of the inconsistency and the effects of threatened self-image. Once these effects are separated, we see that people are really responding to the assault on the self rather than to the norm of consistency.[41]

> There is a near-infinite variety of interchangeable adaptations
> – cognitive and behavioral – to such inconsistencies. Indeed,
> our coping options in everyday life are thus widely varied,
> widely interchangeable, and not restricted by the elements of
> the provoking inconsistency, but only by the requirement that
> they affirm the self.[42]

Steele argues that the flexibility of humans in solving dissonance problems in a variety of ways plays an evolutionarily important role in humans both in coping and in having the capacity to remain objective about themselves. Finally, Steele suggests that much of what seems to the agent and others as cohering behaviors are rationalizations aimed at affirming a positive view of the self rather than a reflection of a genuinely rational self.[43]

Reference to these studies does not prove that consistency and overall coherence of outlook are not important. But it does suggest that what we sometimes like to refer to as an innate drive to theoretical comprehensiveness may not be an accurate portrayal of what drives us behaviorally or cognitively.

CONCLUSION

A moral theory is a model of moral life analogous to the way in which the general theory of relativity is a model of physical geometry. The two sets of data – moral life and physical geometry – are not appropriately modeled along the same lines. All models are simplifications. But the models of moral theory obscure what is central to the phenomena modeled – the culturally and historically embedded nature of moral experience and judgment. Theory also misrepresents the nature of rationality that it expects of its practitioners, human agents. Theory presents a short list of formulas such that if one knew all the facts and could apply the formulas accurately, one would have the key to correct judgment, by a deduction so to speak. In its place, we can suggest the model of constitutional interpretation, as exemplified in the book *American Constitutional Law* by Laurence Tribe.[44] In this domain no set of moral formulas and facts would suffice to lead to a judgment. Instead, it is the evolution of doctrine within specific domains that determines correct outcomes for that jurisdiction. There is no pretense that an outcome appropriate in one jurisdiction would be appropriate in another. Nor is there the pretense that if the formulas were good enough, we would be done with the task. As history and culture change, so do our interpretations.

One of the disturbing implications for the position being advanced here is the relationship of dependency it places us in vis-à-vis our culture. Our prospect of being right about something, especially about something important and fundamental to our outlook, is almost completely a function of our culture's attitude toward that issue. We have little more prospect of being something other than children of our age than we have of being children of other parents. The reasoning that we use to transcend our cultural limitations will be, by and large, reasoning our culture has supplied and that lies latent in its perspective. Pure rationality does not offer us independent standards by which we can gauge the fundamental principles by which we assess our cultural tendencies. Its stamp will be on all we do, on all we think. Its limitations are inevitably ours, and that is our fate. As I have argued, it is also our nature to be culturally enmeshed, and thus what is our limitation is at the same time our saving grace. Moral reflection should be cognizant of this.

This reassessment of culture's role in moral life should focus our attention on the need to reorient moral theory. Instead of replacing culture, moral theory should strive to understand how people gain direction, connection, and meaning from their participation in associations with others. It is not the person as autonomous, cognitively and morally independent, that moral theory should model, but people as limited and interdependent for their most basic needs and directions.[45] Standard accounts of freedom as autonomy obscure this feature of moral character, judgment, and life. Accounts of privacy that fail to focus on its relational nature similarly obscure it. Once this reinterpretation takes hold, the role of privacy in both maintaining and modulating social influences can be made clear.

Chapter 6

Explaining privacy's place

In this chapter, I explain privacy's role in sustaining social freedom. To prepare for that explanation, I first discuss the importance of social control for societies and associations of various sorts and sizes. I then develop an account of social freedom, and end with a discussion of privacy's role in counterbalancing social control mechanisms.

As argued in the past several chapters, there is ample reason to change our conception of moral rationality. The principle of articulated rationality is not well suited to reveal the nature of moral understanding or moral being. The principle's contempt of culture and of our susceptibility to socializing pressures and influences makes it an inappropriate standard for human practices. We are not rational beings in the senses that moral theories often stress: We are not rational in the sense of being primarily or exclusively motivated to further our self-interest independent of all else. We see ourselves as social beings whose stake lies in life with others. We are not rational in the sense that how others do things, how our culture does things, is irrelevant to legitimization. Customary practices are a legitimizing ground. We are not rational in the sense that we should be confident that our own judgment, when not supported by others, is a valid basis for action or judgment. We are not rational in the sense that we need no more motivation for judging or acting than is provided by having an abstract belief that something is right or wrong. We understand ourselves as proper objects of moral or social manipulation, by ourselves and by others.

It is in delineating some of the appropriate forms of such social manipulation that I explain the role of privacy. It is in appreciating our dependence on others and on culture for our outlook and judgment that I elaborate a notion of social freedom that pays homage to our social nature.

In this chapter, I counter the standard picture of social responsiveness – vulnerability to social pressure – as a human impairment and, in so doing, suggest the role privacy plays in facilitating social freedom.

First, a litany of trivialities: Individuals need cultures to survive. But perhaps even deeper than the drive to survive is the need to be part of a human context. The need to be part of a human context can be explained by culture's role in promoting survival. Cultures are standardized habits of perceiving, judging, and acting that reflect accumulated experience.[1] No one could discover enough on his or her own to manage well enough, let alone comparably well, outside the cultural context. Furthermore, as we saw Geertz argue in the preceding chapter, it is erroneous to suppose that the human brain evolved independent of the social context.

Biology has selected for socially adaptive and responsive beings. Human neonates that are deprived of adequate emotional nurturing founder physically as well as emotionally. Infants that do not respond to efforts at social nurturing are much more likely to be neglected or abandoned than are infants born socially responsive. The message is clear: Be socially responsive.[2]

As noted in Chapter 5, strategies connected with sociability and traditions serve a role ignored by those philosophical theories that stress individual autonomy in value orientation. This provides an explanation, but not an available motivation, for reliance on a cultural tradition. The social processes have more overall adaptive value than do particular theoretical reconstructions, which entitles these processes to a defensible authoritative role even under circumstances that initially may make them appear unfounded or even wrong to practitioners of articulated rationality. As long as we can recognize that there are aspects of our strategies that we may not understand, it is reasonable to opt for the strategy-selected outcome rather than some apparently higher-ranked alternative. Our conforming proclivity to traditions can be defended on strategic and other grounds as against rationalist alternatives, even though these traditions cannot be defended satisfactorily on substantive grounds.[3]

We must also recall my argument against the common assumption that all reasons must be reducible to, or justifiable in terms of, first-order reasons. Our basis for finding reasoning acceptable, in terms of both form and content, is based on acceptance of authorities and processes one is not positioned to individually validate. Rather than leading to skepticism, this realization might help us recognize our dependence on authorities, even for critical assessments.

Recognizing our own cognitive and emotional limitations, we face a problem for which there is no neat solution: What happens when we do not understand a standard? We may not have reason to oppose the standard but still not comprehend its basis. Alternatively we may have personal reasons or even just feelings for opposing it. Or we may notice that there is a conflict in relevant standards, whether or not we understand their bases. Any response to this situation that recommended acting only on what one could understand for oneself would be sociopathic. A given person may not understand what is wrong with child molesting. Another may not be able to articulate a basis for refraining from harming others when expedient. What can advocates of autonomy suggest in these cases?

We should be skeptical of the adequacy of rational reconstructions of human social judgment. Just as economic models of rationality seem oblivious to concerns that people take very seriously,[4] rational reconstructions of morality may miss what is most central to moral life, as explained in Chapter 5. Philosophers have no difficulty identifying failure of *normative* economic models when these models fail to fit what we find important. Yet many do not follow the same course in their assessment of standard moral models.[5]

Group processes that involve conforming tendencies facilitate social life. There is a powerful tendency for people to conform to group processes, and this phenomenon has become an obsession, occasioning a cascade of fascinating studies about conformity under conditions of individual reservation.[6]

Once we acknowledge the significance of conformity to cultural life, matters become complicated in ways that I do not think are widely enough appreciated by critics of conformity. Cultures and traditions go a long way toward settling how a person will frame his or her experiences of the world.[7] Cultures and traditions will also impose values, loyalties, framing effects,[8] and directions on the members of these cultures. Although we like to say that people are responsible for the values they adopt from the cultures they inhabit, there is something peculiar about this way of putting it. The peculiarity lies in the failure to see that culture and traditions have *authority* for people, and this authority means that individuals are not, and do not see themselves as, entirely free to pick and choose among cultural norms what is worth embodying in their own lives. If people in fact approach a tradition in the spirit of selective and reasoned embrace and rejection, it is fair to say that the culture or tradition is not one they feel part of and is not one that has authority for them. Surely part of feeling that a tradition has authority for one is thinking that it has embedded in it resources rich enough to transcend what one can fully plumb.

Any notion of personal identity involves situating the individual within a cultural context that goes a long way toward framing the individual's outlook and values. Because it is critical that people position themselves within a tradition or culture, we must accept that they will come to see as appropriate some behavior or styles that people outside the tradition find enigmatic, troublesome, or misguided. We recognize that they will not approach all issues as ones to be settled by an objective, culturally neutral perspective, or if they do aim to do this, it will be at considerable psychic expense. Let me illustrate. John Wideman is a very successful and talented American writer. He makes clear in his autobiographical account that his own rejection of ghetto values as he was growing up had enormous costs for him. It cut him off from the vision, riches and pains, sense of rage, that he identifies as central to the African-American experience, and thus from a part of himself.[9] Wideman explores the differences between his brother, serving a life sentence for murder, and himself. He discovers in himself a receptivity or appreciation for the sort of rebellious life, outlook, and intelligence he locates in his bother but that he, the author, rejected early in his own development. He recognizes a sense of dignity he did not know existed in the life he abandoned. He learns that to achieve success and respectability, he incorporated the values that debase and disenfranchise the people he is closest to. As we learn more about the role and requirements of cultural identification, I believe we shall also appreciate the limited extent of an abstract or culturally alien ethical or rational scheme's authority over people's lives.

Learning and judgment presuppose trust in certain authorities: parents, teachers, community leaders, elected officials, religious leaders. It also presupposes placing trust in the common behavior patterns one sees around oneself. These routes to social learning and social being are indispensable. Our cognitive and moral economies require that we rely on such authorities for the bulk of our everyday judgments. No one occupies the Olympian perspective from which her own culture can be evaluated objectively. Cultures promote self-criticism and examination, to varying degrees, but these too are culturally conditioned processes.

In some circles, it is taken for granted that what is authentic in individuals comprises ends that are independent of social ends. The widespread attractions of contractualism in moral and political philosophy illustrate this. Indifference to, and independence from, others are taken as natural and fundamental to human nature, whereas concern and social participation are seen as strategies motivated by appeal to maximizing prospects for self-advancement.[10] Authenticity can be restored only by reducing the vulnerability of individuals to socially formative, and thus manipulative, influences. This is the principal concern behind the appeal of articulate rationality.

There is an alternative perspective elaborated by George Herbert Mead according to which human nature itself derives from socialization, and that the organization of mind that is necessary for self, self-interest, and criticism is itself a function of social organization internalized. For Mead, the very ability to adopt the perspective of the other through rule-governed patterns of interaction makes possible self-criticism, self-regulation, cooperation, and social criticism.[11]

> Hence, social control, so far from tending to crush out the human individual or to obliterate his self-conscious individuality, is, on the contrary, actually constitutive of and inextricably associated with that individuality; for the individual is what he is, as a conscious and individual personality, just in as far as he is a member of society, involved in the social process of experience and activity, and thereby socially controlled in his conduct.[12]

Our peculiarly human traits are not threatened by recognition of the role of culture and peer pressure on our lives. We are social beings, and have our culture to credit for both our ability to manage life with others and for the critical perspective by which we look at our culture.

I go on now to discuss the constructive role of social pressure, its place in securing social freedom, and then the role of privacy in establishing domains of social freedom.

MORALLY GAUGING SOCIAL PRESSURES

Conformity is a powerful human impulse and prerequisite to living life together. One can have substantive grounds to change this or that particular cultural practice, but one cannot have substantive grounds for validating a cultural outlook wholesale. Mill, as we saw in Chapter 2, argued that an individual's proper motivational structure is one that resonated only with certain sorts of reasons. This vision of the control of the rational seems to be an occupational hazard to which philosophers succumb. Is it legitimate for a culture to capitalize on people's vulnerability to social pressure to nudge people in the right direction, even in areas where we think that they have the right to go in the wrong direction? A "nudge" is a reason that does not relate directly to the substance of the decision but to some other motivating factor, like social approval. Or is it incumbent on societies to aim to move in the direction Mill suggested, renouncing nonrational appeals to the forms of life that define them? Let's take a simple example. Becoming and remaining politically informed is important but a bother, and sometimes unpleasant or depressing. So, we have reason to stay informed and we have reason not to. Realizing that the reasons we have to become slack here may be more alluring than the reasons we have to remain attentive, we might want to endorse the use of social approval or stigmatization as a way of tipping the motivational scales on behalf of staying informed.

However, there may be people who agree about the value of being politically informed but find it wrong that there be any additional incentive, one unrelated to the intrinsic merits, for engaging in this behavior. They might urge that if keeping abreast of the political context is not important enough in someone's personal economy of values to win on its own merits, it is manipulative, and hence inappropriate, to foster this interest through fear of social disapproval or stigma or, more positively, through a system of social rewards.

What is at issue is a way of life and a motivational structure that a community promotes. It is hard to see what it means to say that the community endorses something unless this is connected to social attitudes that disapprove of alternative courses in varying degrees. We must recognize that social pressure to conform to standards that cannot be individually or collectively established is what it is that ties people to one another within a way of life. In many societies dissenters may try to persuade others that the social norm ought to be different from what it is, and such efforts are often regarded as contributing to the stature of the critic, even when unsuccessful. It would be unrealistic to assume, however, that the community (in a social but not political sense) has a responsibility to promote only those values that it can rationally defend, or limit its form of influence to presentation of the merit of a cause to motivate individual conformity. An association that never engaged feelings of group solidarity to encourage conforming or right behavior would hardly count as a human society and would prove extremely unstable over time. In a community that differentiates legal and political norms from social norms, the sorts of control mechanisms available to communities will inevitably include social pressure.[13]

Alternatively, someone might argue that because keeping abreast politically is the responsible thing to do, social pressures that move people in that direction are not manipulative. Here I am only concerned that we recognize the important role social pressures have to play in maintaining a society, not with whether we call it manipulative. I will argue that social pressures play an important role in establishing and maintaining social freedom.

Finally, an austere view of rational control would fail to acknowledge forms of support that we know people need. It is obvious that people in trouble fare better when they know that there is support for their efforts. In such contexts it would be wrong of us to deny support because we felt that it would appeal to and indirectly support nonrational deliberative and motivational features of human life. It follows that people are not rational in the narrow sense that would prohibit all appeals except those made with objective reasons that make no reference to what others think of one. Human lives or social well-being would be impoverished if we would wean people from their natural motivational structure that considers other people's attitudes.

In contemplating enforcement of norms, societies are different from political bodies. Arguments that are appropriate for explaining why the criminal law should not be employed to achieve certain ends do not necessarily also apply to informally "enforced" community norms. Society's enforcement mechanisms are limited but include powerful in-centives like community inclusion or exclusion, application of a spectrum of social gradings involving notions of honor and shame, and differentiated expenditures of social support resources. So where Mill and others have sought to liberate people from the forms of pressure that undermine articulate rationality, we must recognize the significance of these pres-sures for social organization and effectiveness.[14]

While the state, through its criminal law, should take the perspective that all of the citizens are to be equally protected, the community norms might be more parochial in outlook. Those who violate its central norms need not be treated as equal members of the community. It need not take the same rational stance as the liberal state does. It would be a violation of the very associational rights we find enhancing of liber-alism and privacy to require communities to abide by the rules fitting for the state. Nonpolitical communities will have different constitutions than will the political community.

This recognition leaves us with the problem that in certain contexts, private organizations are enough like the state – they perform so many of the same functions as the political community – that we might think it incumbent on them to act like the state with regard to neutrality.

I wish to emphasize the necessary role of associations that lie between the individual and the state. Few would dispute the critical role of such mid-level communities, varying widely as they do in size, structure, and objectives. It is primarily, if not solely, through these ties that one becomes effective as a social actor. Yet philosophers pay little attention to organizational strategies that are inevitably necessary for these associations to garner loyalty, establish authority over an individual, maintain organization, and facilitate their op-eration. What is important for human freedom is not the independence from associational pressures that Mill feared. What is critical instead is the limited scope of any given associational tie, combined with the variety of directions of-fered the individual by the diversity of associational roles.[15]

Individuals need both social organization and associational

ties to act effectively in a safe social context. Both the society at large and the particular organizations through which individuals express their wills require social pressures to maintain themselves and act effectively. When these social pressures of any particular association are limited by alternative sources of support for individuals and their projects, by the presence of alternative associations, then we have met one of the conditions of social freedom.

Let me contrast this condition of social freedom with that view promoted by Mill. For Mill one is socially free so long as one does not in fact succumb to intimidations of social reproach. A social system is socially free when generally an individual is not socially punished for self-regarding behavior, beliefs, and attitudes, however unpopular. On the view I am presenting, social freedom is grounded in availability of alternative systems of social support for individual and group projects. I regard social reproach as a socially and associationally necessary means by which social groups maintain structure, direction, and effectiveness. Through participation in associations, social beings make their will effective in the world. Without the help of others, typically but not always in organized settings, most of what we think of as individual objectives would not be possible or even conceivable. This is why from my perspective social freedom is enhanced by the very processes Mill thought anathema to it.

Social pressures, in contrast to rational arguments, play a role at two different points: at the point of original value and character formation and at the point of altering a particular decision at which a fully formed person arrives. (Undoubtedly, it is preferable to see these "points" as occurring on a spectrum of social influences.) In altering a decision, it can provide information that is issue-focused, or it can provide reasons that are external to the merits of the decision problem. Even though on its "merits" it was decided one way, an extra kick is given to ensure its grip or to swing it another way.

This "extra kick" or nudge, the social incentive, does not inevitably undermine anything important. If we were perfectly confident about our own ability to judge on merits and abide by judgment, then we might see the extra kick as gratuitous or demeaning. Given our imperfections as deliberators and actors, we may find that the extra kick is an indispensable and valued aspect of keeping ourselves on a course that makes life with others feasible.[16] Aristotle claimed that one of the values of the best type of friendship is that it helps sustain an interest in worthy ends. He recognized that even the worthiest of ends did not sustain motivation. Sabini and Silver describe a phenomenon they label "moral drift."[17] Moral drift occurs when people lose confidence in their values because they see little public recognition or support for these values in the public culture.

Some writers are sympathetic to *individuals'* committing themselves to acting in ways that are not rational, because thereby they generate opportunities unavailable to those not so committed. The standard example used in the literature is marriage. By structuring marriage commitments so that they are hard to break, we interfere with people doing what they want to do, but in so doing enable them to relate in ways, have enduring relationships, that would otherwise be more difficult or impossible.

When it comes to social groups, however, we demand standards of rationality that preclude such enabling strategies. To the extent that you disallow reference to traditions and authorities in justifying or legitimizing social action or group change, you preclude higher-order considerations, despite the possibility that such considerations, and consideration for what cannot always be explicitly articulated, may enable possibilities that are otherwise inaccessible.[18]

A clear example of this problem, cited by Jon Elster, has to do with rights. So long as rights are respected for instrumental reasons, citizens will worry that circumstances may change, and the reasons that formerly spoke in favor of rights now provide the basis for their recision. So for rights to be effective, there must be assurances that they will be maintained even though there is a better argument for their annulment.[19]

Cognizant of our rational limitations and social dependence, we cannot make as clear-cut a moral distinction as we might have liked between deciding something on its merits and acting because of social pressures. Even the expression "deciding something on its merits" oversimplifies the case, because it presupposes that fitting in with others or acting as others expect is no virtue, and carries with it no credit. It is as if finding intrinsic value in a group process is equated with behaving like a robot.

We readily recognize the importance of having laws that threaten punishment as a means of channeling behavior patterns in the right direction. Why is taking account of individual imperfections legitimate in political and personal rationality but illegitimate in social rationality?[20]

We can distinguish different sorts of social failings, arguing that social pressure is appropriate for some but not others, and is appropriate for some associations but not others. For instance, one could plausibly suggest that social pressure is more apt when a person needs extra motivation to do what he or she already regards as the thing to do, like exercise, and less fitting if the individual endorses different values.[21] That may be conceded without undermining the value of social pressure. Think about cases where out of laziness a person goes on holding beliefs such that were he to consider them, he would revise them. Because this person believes that his beliefs are correct, he is not motivated to reconsider them, and consequently he does not appreciate the reasons *he would have* to confront his values.

Recall John Stuart Mill's discussion of social pressure that we reviewed in Chapter 2. Mill argued that in those domains of life where we have no moral right to expect something of a person, we may reason with him, we may find that we do not wish to associate with him, but we may not engage in any retributive or specifically punitive response, objective or emotional. As I noted, this standard would undermine important group dynamics that are responsible for the cohesion and effectiveness of social groups. The effectiveness of groups, in turn, enables individuals to have social impact, to be effective social agents. Philosophers have not questioned Mill on his standard because they have not focused on people's relationships to groups.

What does social pressure mean and what does it encompass? Is the existence of a social norm itself a form of social pressure? We have to distinguish between different types of pressures. I think that in normal parlance we would not say that merely informing a person of a good reason for doing something is a way of putting pressure on that person, though if combined, even tacitly, with other messages it would be. Suppose we find that women who drink alcohol during pregnancy experience a 50 percent increased risk of birth defects compared with women who do not drink. Is publicizing this information a form of pressure? Dissemination of this information would clearly be meant to do one or both of the following: (1) provide pregnant women with information so that *they* could decide whether the risk is legitimate in light of their values, (2) socially increase the costs – for instance by stigmatizing women who drink alcohol while pregnant – so that pregnant women will not drink. The closer we come to the second method, the closer we are to exploiting social pressure. To take a more clearly self-regarding form of behavior, consider smoking. Everyone knows that smoking causes cancer. That information is ineffective in millions of cases. But socially, the costs of smoking are increasing in that smokers are informed that fewer and fewer facilities and people will tolerate smoking. So smokers come to feel out of place and have a new incentive to quit – social acceptance.

Other examples from the social domain will help show conclusively that social pressure in the form of social condemnation or social punishment is at times a fitting response outside the domain of criminal law, and even outside the domain of moral duties. Suppose a neighbor driving by sees me walking, in a torrential downpour one mile from my house, with heavy grocery bags. Suppose further that he even stops his car to remark how the paper shopping bags I am carrying are coming apart because of the rain. But he does not offer me a lift. How could someone think that resentment is not an appropriate response on my part? Here it is important to notice that the reaction is not just of the form, "if this is what this fellow does, I do not want to be part of his life." The reaction will be infused with a sense of fitting anger. This is so even though we would not think this person owes me a ride or owes it to me to be a more considerate person. Some Jews, even nonreligious ones, react with resentment against other Jews who convert or, what in their opinion is worse, become a "Jew for Jesus." They see this as betrayal and feel intense resentment. Similarly, members of many ethnic communities may feel resentment when others abandon "their roots" for the social acceptance and upward mobility that goes with assimilation. People with various disabilities may feel resentment toward others with similar disabilities who chose to discontinue life-sustaining treatment. They feel betrayed or devalued because of others' decisions that their (the others') lives are not worth living. Knowing that this emotional outcome is likely motivates people to some extent to stay loyal to a group by putting a higher price on defection. On Millian principles we would have to say about these latter cases that no one else has a right to feel that this person owes it to them that they not convert religiously or culturally. Rather than think that the typical resentful reaction is wrongminded, I think that Mill and others failed to appreciate what psychological resources groups, whether voluntary or not, require to think of themselves and act as associations or communities.[22]

Associations clearly act as if they need some control mechanism over members to be effective. An acquaintance of mine recently told me of an instance of this perceived need. She was a member of a group of black women scholars. She showed other members of this group a paper she had written and wanted to publish. Because the other members of the group found the paper to have the potential of further undermining social confidence in blacks, they urged her not to publish. The acquaintance understood that she then had the choice of publishing the article and alienating herself from the group of people she admired and depended on for support or remaining silent on something she believed worthy of exposure and maintaining her relationship with supportive and powerful allies.

In a similar vein is a policy of the National Association for the Advancement of Colored People. That policy states that when the national office endorses or opposes something, local offices may not take opposing stands. The NAACP realizes that for its voice to be as effective as possible, it cannot be contradicted by opposing voices claiming to represent the same constituency.

In each of these instances we feel that a heavy-handed approach has been used. Nevertheless, it is easy to appreciate the sense of necessity both in the informal and in the formal organizational operations. This is not to say that anything an association feels it needs to be effective should be excused. Few people would find kidnapping and brainwashing of people to be legitimate means for organizations to maintain control. Some dynamic factors can help us assess what is legitimate, or at least what will be judged as such.

Recall our discussion of Mill in which we saw him treat as legitimate only reference to the merit of a position and not to social aspects of a belief or value. Because we, as self-consciously imperfect rational agents and social beings, would want such techniques of social control to be available, we must part with Mill on this point. We want such techniques to be available, I suggest, because we know that associations, and with them the prospects of effective human agency, would disappear without them.

What we do not have is a decision procedure, at either the individual or social level, for telling when reliance on authority, tradition, or practice in the face of apparently good argument is wrong or inefficient. Whereas philosophy, like decision theory, has often sought to offer an approach that could address this problem mechanically, the resources it offers for managing the problem have been restricted to narrow, first-order considerations, reflected in the principle of articulate rationality. In considering the limitations of this approach, I am not suggesting abandonment of criticism and action based on reason. I am suggesting instead that modesty about our capacity to model and project outcomes of change is appropriate.

When does social pressure become subversive? If a person refrains from killing or maiming, in part, because of concern for others' opinions of him, has the response reflected overbearing social pressure? If I don't personally see what is so wrong with an incestuous relationship with my preadolescent children, yet refrain from this because of concern for the harsh judgment of my friends, has the pressure been overbearing? In cases like these, we may think that there is no real possibility for too much pressure. What can happen as a result of these pressures is that the deviant will come to see things differently over time, not because of an argument, but because of effective resocialization. Such examples highlight the strongest case for the virtue of social pressures: pressures designed for people who would on their own violate central values of respect for life and trust.

Let us take some examples in the self-regarding domain. I may feel strongly tempted to smoke. Is it worrisome for someone disposed in this way to feel pressured into having a healthier life, when on its own the merits of this style do not inspire excitement? In addressing this question, we should differentiate cases where without social pressure people would waste their lives and cases where people would have perfectly wonderful but nonstandard lives. By and large, social pressures will discourage both, and depending on what one anticipates as the ratio of these two possibilities, and the harm engendered by each, one will tend to approve or disapprove of varying degrees and modes of social pressures.

Assessing what level of pressure impinges on a person is a judgment that involves assessing several factors in addition to the strength of the pressure. The difference between overreaching and legitimate social pressure cannot be assessed in terms of the comparative level of the pressures by itself. There could be more pressure to avoid A than there is to avoid B, even though the amount of pressure to do B is overreaching and the amount of pressure to do A is not. For instance, we might suggest that *any* pressure to avoid B, say, engaging in sex with one's spouse, is overreaching, whereas a good deal of pressure is appropriate for avoiding A, say, marching with the Nazis or Klan.

This point about the complexities of assessing social pressure as overreaching can be illustrated by the notion of coercion. The concept of coercion is relevant here because it too is used as a way of gauging whether a person's behavior reflects or is an expression of the person's will. An intricate array of reasons is relevant to assessing whether an agent, in making a choice, is to be regarded as the author of the decision. Compare: I agree to sell you my house for $10,000 because you threaten to slash my face unless I do so. In a wartime setting, after being captured by the enemy to avoid being summarily executed I agree to make no effort to escape. Although the prospect of death is more fearsome than the prospect of a scarred face, the latter agreement is more binding than the former, less an undermining of the agent's real will. In part, this assessment is a result of the fact that the enemy had the right to confront me with the choice of death or agreement, whereas the potential purchaser of my house had no right to confront me with the choice of $10,000 for my house or a slashed face.[23]

The concept of overreaching can also be likened to the notion of being careful. There is no one level of attention that counts as being careful enough in all activities. Different levels of care are required for different sorts of behavior and with different sorts of potential consequences.

The concept of overreaching in the context of the criminal law has been vigorously and voluminously addressed. There, Mill's criterion of "harm to others" has been the object of conceptual and normative analysis. Many distinguished writers are on record defending both the spirit and letter of Mill's approach to the limits of legal coercion. Mill and his defenders understandably sought clear and rigorous standards for legal intervention. As mentioned in the chapter on Mill, it has been taken for granted by liberal writers that just as it is possible to present clear standards for legal intervention, it is possible to present clear standards for social pressure. The position here amounts to arguing that social pressure, especially when divorced from rational arguments, is always out of place. As we saw, this was the position Mill dedicated himself to advancing in *On Liberty*. This position seemed attractive to writers, especially philosophers, who found themselves professionally committed to locating the dignity of people in their rationality and independence.

I am here denying the plausibility of this approach to social pressure. I am advocating the appropriateness of social pressure in the absence of rational articulation establishing the rightness of one's outlook. I am denying that there is any precise and universal standard for assessing when social pressure is apt. I am not denying that there is some structure to the issue. This and the next chapter have the burden of suggesting what that structure is. The contours of norms related to social overreaching can be elaborated best in the context of a discussion of privacy.

The upshot of this variable standard of social overreaching is that the domains in which privacy rightly shields people from social pressure is itself variable. Where it is important for people to explore and express their own private life, or to pursue objectives in an association with others, privacy shields people from some forms of social pressure.

Our notion of privacy is more ramified than surface grammar makes explicit. Normally we say something is private or it is not. This dichotomy obscures several contextual features that can be made explicit. And normally we think about privacy as privacy vis-à-vis certain people or groups. This tendency obscures the fact that privacy also has a "for something" and "with someone" dimension. A privacy attribution pertains to certain subjects (S), is about certain matters (M), is relative to certain people (P), in certain roles (R), in certain contexts (C), and typically for certain associational objectives (O). Characteristically, we need to know what O is to appreciate the form of the privacy relationship. For instance, many aspects of my (S) marriage (M) are private vis-à-vis Norman (P), my student (R), during the normal course of events (C) in order that I may have a special relationship with my wife (O). Variations in any of the terms indicated could change the plausibility of the claim. Certain terms of association legitimate or even require access to parts of selves that other associative terms preclude, and the elaboration of the norms of privacy helps us monitor how this is so. Implicit in our privacy claims is this understanding of the variable terms of this structure. Belonging to a community legitimizes access to one by other members over a range of matters that define the community. We can use religious community as an example. Although we tend to regard religion as a private or personal domain of self, within many religious communities it is regarded as fitting for members to help one another improve their spiritual lives through a variety of supportive mechanisms. Among some groups of Southern Baptists, for instance, there is no appropriate role for a sense of privacy or individuality with regard to matters religious – and this encompasses almost everything – within the religious community.[24] I go on now to explain some of the factors that seem relevant to calibrating rightful from overreaching social pressure.[25]

A NATURAL HISTORY OF PRIVACY

In Chapter 1, I distinguished between two different institutions of privacy, one encouraging self-expression and the other not. Both preclude in some measure access or information about people and, as such, sustain a sense of propriety and dignity related to human encounters. What I called expressive-role privacy also serves the purpose of giving individuals (or groups) scope for unsupervised self-expression. It is this latter sense of privacy that I will discuss here. Privacy related to private life protects people from social overreaching so that they can explore dimensions of life in a relatively unconstrained manner. Still, this sort of privacy, like the other, is association-relative. That is, some behavior or information can be private vis-à-vis some people or groups and not vis-à-vis others. You do not overstep your parents' privacy when *you* ask them things that would surely be out of bounds for *me* to meddle into.

Some of the factors that determine what counts as social overreaching and hence define the contours of privacy include material security, social differentiation, and the feasibility of self-conscious social engineering. In providing a theory of overreaching, I introduce a speculative natural history of privacy.

I mentioned that people inevitably depend on groups, social associations, for material, spiritual, and cultural needs. But the nature, function, and extent of the groups, and hence the nature of the dependence, change over time. In times of lesser material abundance and greater insecurity, associations were less specialized than today, and correspondingly the associations that were operative encompassed more aspects of a person's life. There were fewer distinct areas of life than is the case with us that were out of bounds with respect to the group's sphere of relevance and dependence. Quoting Simmel:

> The earliest phase of social formations found in historical as well as in contemporary social structures is this: a relatively small circle firmly closed against neighboring, strange, or in some way antagonistic circles. However, this circle is closely coherent and allows its individual members only a narrow field for the development of unique qualities and free, self-responsible movements. Political and kinship groups, parties and religious associations begin in this way. The self-preservation of very young associations requires the establishment of strict boundaries and a centripetal unity. Therefore they cannot allow the individual freedom and unique inner and outer development. . . .
> The ancient *polis* in this respect seems to have had the very

character of a small town. The constant threat to its existence at the hands of enemies from near and afar effected strict coherence in political and military respects, a supervision of the citizen by the citizen, a jealousy of the whole against the individual whose particular life was suppressed to such a degree that he could compensate only by acting as a despot in his own household.[26]

With less rapidly changing social and material environments, associations would not have had to be as flexible and committed to participant input as they are today. Change could occur by evolutionary processes that afforded little scope to conscious engineering. Social structures were regarded as ordered by nature, not by collective decision. Social structures that were in place would have been time-tested and were not very responsive to individually initiated alterations. The adaptive processes could afford to be slower to respond to environmental changes, because there were fewer changes that had not been encountered before. In this context, people would place little value on individual innovation or criticism. Correspondingly less value would be accorded to aspects of self that were out of harmony with the dominant social outlook than is the case today. Societies that feel themselves threatened tend to insist on and experience higher levels of social solidarity. Earlier societies may have felt more threatened by individual deviations and innovations than today's societies, because they were in fact more dependent on dominant, unifying features of culture to keep them afloat. Both formal studies and everyday experience present convincing evidence that under conditions of anxiety, people find comfort in association with others.[27]

Where the material and cultural climates encounter rapid flux, the social evolution of groups becomes too slow. Change mechanisms have to be self-consciously embraced as conducive to social survival. This consciousness affords greater value to individual initiative and outlook as affording the group a means of coping. As individual initiative became more important for social viability, the balance of what is legitimately expected of the individual changes, and with it the place on the spectrum that is identified with social over-reaching.

As a way of adapting to the need for change, associations of a more specialized nature will take over many of the roles that global association or community provided in more precarious times. The emerging functionality and multiplication of groups result in less individual dependence on any specific group and of any group on any specific individual. So as individuals and groups, one by one, become more independent of one another, there will be less pressure to be part of any given group, and there will be more definition or specificity in the terms of the relationships within any group.[28] Membership in a society will not hinge on belonging to "the" group, but instead on belonging to some selection of groups that have certain family resemblances and interdependencies.

It is worthwhile suggesting *how* it is, or in what sense it is, that the independence of various associations that result from cultural differentiation liberate the individual. It is not just the result of the freedom of association that increases over time. It is also the result of the ends of the associations themselves coming to take on a heightened status independent of the general social welfare. Over time the law of entropy applies to value: Autonomous value is increasingly found distributed in many goods, not just in the monolithic, hierarchically structured good. Such a less structured concatenation of goods diminishes the standing or right of any one centralized good to represent the standard by which all issues are judged. No one value outlook always dominates, and moral authority is invested in many value principalities. Each of these value principalities, associations, claims authority,[29] but few have the power to cripple seriously those who opt out.

This picture of freedom as enhanced freedom of association is entirely compatible with, and is in fact dependent upon, individual groups having at their disposal social enforcement mechanisms – access to social pressures – to maintain themselves. Privacy is just as important for the group to maintain its integrity and independence as it is for the individual to maintain her integrity and independence.[30]

Historical circumstances force different relationships between individuals and social groups. Some of these enhance the role of the individual outlook and diversify the terms of individual association. Both of these directions afford more scope for privacy. Groups, as I have said, become less dependent on conformity and more dependent on individual variation and outlook as sources of change. As these dependencies lessen, what it is fair for the community to expect of the individual lessens or at least narrows. And as the community's role in shaping the individual and promoting survival and transmission of strategies for common life becomes distributed among more restricted functional associations, more relationships will arise from which aspects of people's lives become irrelevant or less critical. This then, like the emerging dependence on individual variation, fosters privacy, for it affords less basis for others to have access to various parts of people's lives. As it becomes less critical for social viability that others be able to control various dimensions of an individual's life, then forms of control that were legitimate become illegitimate. Aspects of communitywide control that were appropriate move into the overreaching zone.[31]

In an illuminating discussion of the historical-cultural processes I am describing, Georg Simmel states the following:

> The association based on some particular interest is the discreet sociological form *par excellence*. Its members are psychologically anonymous. In order to form the association, all they have to know of one another is precisely this fact – that they form it. The increasing objectification of our culture, whose phenomena consist more and more of impersonal elements and less and less absorb the subjective totality of the individual (most simply shown by the contrast between handicraft and factory work), also involves sociological structures. Therefore, groups into which earlier man entered in his totality and individuality and which, for this reason, required reciprocal knowledge far

111

beyond the immediate, objective content of the relationship –
these groups are now based exclusively on this objective content, which is neatly factored out of the whole relation. . . .

The objectification of culture has decisively differentiated the
quanta of knowledge and ignorance necessary for confidence.
The modern merchant who enters business with another; the
scholar who together with another embarks upon an investigation; the leader of a political party who makes an agreement
with the leader of another party concerning matters of election
or the treatment of pending bills; all these know . . . only exactly *that* and no more about their partner which they *have* to
know for the sake of the relationship they wish to enter. The
traditions and institutions, the power of public opinion and
the definition of the position which inescapably stamps the
individual, have become so solid and reliable that one has to
know only certain external facts about the other person in order
to have the confidence required for the common action. . . .
Under more primitive, less differentiated conditions, the individual knows much more about his partner in regard to
personal matters, and much less in regard to his purely objective competence.[32]

In this analysis of modern associations or groups, individuals become members on an increasingly specialized basis,
mirroring the increasingly specialized function of associations. This means, in turn, that people one associates with
have only a very narrow range of behaviors that constitute
"their business," their field of legitimate concern. So nearly
everything one does is accessible without overreaching to
some people, but almost nothing one does is accessible without overreaching to most. The division of labor among associations and the alternatives for associations even with a
given function provide each individual with a basis for choice
without crippling consequences.

I mentioned the possibility of a society's carrying out many
or most of the functions we count on the state to perform
and asked whether the appropriate privacy norms would be
those of the state or those of the society. In conditions of
relatively little social differentiation or specialization we can
surmise that little about people will be inaccessible to others

and respect for self-expression will be low. The factors that connect people will be so extensive that there will be relatively little individuals can treat as functionally out of bounds for others.[33]

The account of privacy provided here is a functional account. It engages norms of privacy to enable individuals to develop in ways not subject to overreaching social pressures. It has not begun by positing an intrinsically rightful domain or direction of individual development but has instead treated the scope and extent for legitimate social access to a person as a function of several contextual factors. The thesis has been that qualities of individuals that are promoted in liberal societies are only feasible in materially secure, functionally articulated, self-consciously adaptive social structures. Because what counts as expressing the individual's self and what counts as overreaching interference with this self vary with context and domain, what is rightfully the individual's will vary. Accordingly, what privacy legitimately protects will vary.

Implicit in the account offered is the recognition that it is not just individuals with legitimate private lives that emerge from the historical process. Groups or associations that are less encompassing than the society also emerge, and these also have private lives in a sense. Just as there are group pressures for individuals to conform, there are social pressures on groups to conform to some social standard, and concerns about overreaching are warranted in their case too. The same circumstances that promote individual freedom will be conducive to associational freedoms. And just as it will sometimes be fitting for associations to resist pressures from more encompassing groups, sometimes individuals will legitimately resist pressures from small, intimate associations that might claim too much. The same factors that lead to recognition of smaller voluntary associations lead to recognition of personal residuals in any association. Any group, however small, can be guilty of overreaching in certain situations. Assessing when associational pressures are overreaching will involve the same process sketched already in describing social overreaching generally. Some of the dynamics that make this residual element of people significant are well explored by others.[34] The point here is that privacy is just as necessary in private contexts as it is in social settings.

I have been arguing that it is only in certain sorts of contexts that privacy and individuality will emerge as feasible and desirable social categories. There are important relationships between the structure of groups and the structure of personalities that are potential members of these groups. The same circumstances that engender individuals with privacy needs and private goals will spawn groups that have privacy needs and private goals. It is to these circumstances, associations, and correlated values that individuals are indebted for social and political freedoms. This freedom does not consist in the absence of social pressure from within any group but from the limited role any one group plays in a life, from the existence of a variety of alternative groups that fill the same social role, and from the emergence of value entropy described previously – the reorganization of value from a strictly hierarchical to a composite system of value.

Chapter 7

The ascent of privacy:
a historical and conceptual account

In the preceding chapter, I situated the prospects for social freedom in the domain of a certain social structure. This same structure, I claimed, invokes practices of privacy and group pressures to ensure the integrity of the various associations through which people become free social agents. The chapter ended with a speculative discussion of the social dynamics that would give rise to the kinds of groups that can enable social freedom to emerge as a value.

One immediate implication is that the practice of privacy (of the expressive-role sort) evolves only in certain historical contexts. I suggested that this sort of privacy evolves only when there is a high degree of social and economic specialization, when this specialization liberates individuals from dependence on any group, and where social welfare and security come to depend as much on individual initiative as on cultural rigidity. I illustrate in the present chapter that there is a considerable body of evidence – controversial, theoretical, and speculative though much of it is – to the effect that privacy as a social category emerges only under these conditions.[1] If this claim can be sustained, it means that moral character and the way social life is morally experienced are historically conditioned. To the extent that our moral character is historically conditioned, then, as I argued in Chapter 5, a fundamental presupposition of current moral theory – that human nature is revealed rationally, not historically – is wrong.

This chapter focuses our attention on Western cultural history, because that history is most accessible, and the one we do the least damage to by reading our own values back into. I trace, in rough chronological order, the processes and institutions that gave rise to a constellation of values associated with privacy. We shall see that the breakdown of monolithic value, or what I call value entropy, is associated historically with the emergence of choices among associations. Although this breakdown is usually associated with individualism, the individualism that emerges is one that depends on the various associational options for its fulfillment. I end the chapter with some remarks about the moral relevance of that history.

The etymology of "privacy" provides insight into its connotations in one historical context. "Private," the *Oxford English Dictionary* informs us, derives from the Latin *privatus* meaning "withdrawn from public life" or "deprived of office," and stems from the verb, *privare* meaning "to deprive" or "bereave." In contrast, the word "public" stems from *pubes* referring to adult males, suggesting the locus of decision making. The attitudes toward privacy this etymology suggests were shared by classical Greek culture. Hannah Arendt characterized the private realm as one in which people managed their material dependencies but not their creative, rational, and specifically human dimensions, these latter being the exclusive province of public life.[2]

Cultural historians inform us that much of what we would treat as private the Romans found no reason whatsoever to be reserved about.[3] For instance, on the tombstones of Romans, often placed along the highways, surviving relatives addressed passersby with announcements, like the announcement of a father that the girl entombed was disinherited, or that of a mother announcing that another woman poisoned the boy. Little evidence of the sanctity we associate with death is evidenced in these expressions. Romans generally were fond of exposing wrongdoing in public, and public censure of private conduct was ubiquitous. For instance, individual pride and honor in the face of a wife's infidelity were maintained by public reprimand of the woman's misdeeds. Although Roman law did not in fact transgress all boundaries, there was no obligation to stay clear of any domain of life. What limits there were were not occasioned by norms of privacy.

Not only was the distinction between private and public law very different in ancient Rome than it is with us, but the responsibilities and rights of public officials demonstrate very different conceptions about the relationship between a public trust and a private aspiration. What we would treat as embezzlement of public funds was typically a privilege of office holding. On the other hand, high offices obliged their holders to provide extravagant public benefits, like buildings or festivals, at personal expense. Such largesse was a means by which a man could enhance his prestige.[4]

We see from this sketch that the private–public dichotomy in ancient times was not associated with respect for the private. Nor was it the domain of self-expression. Rather the reverse was the case. This was so not just for domestic activities but for traits or practices associated with action outside the context of public life. As Georges Duby explains it, even through the Middle Ages, solitary wandering was regarded as a symptom of insanity.

> Men and women who traveled the roads without escort were believed to offer themselves up as prey, so it was legitimate to take everything they had. In any case, it was pious work to place them back in some community, regardless of what they might say, to restore them by force to that clearly ordered and well-mannered world where God intended them to be.[5]

Domestic virtues and what we call private morality only slowly evolved in the lives of people who were socially vulnerable and lacked access to traditional forms of power. The focus on domestic order, including fidelity between spouses, obedience of servants, expressions of mutual support and fair dealings between those similarly situated offered stability, community, and security to the lives of many. For the emerging Christian communities, sexual repression constituted the most salient means by which Christians could set themselves apart from their pagan neighbors, being possessed of fewer identifying cultural markers than were the Jews of the period.[6]

In his remarkable two-volume book entitled *The Civilizing Process*, Norbert Elias provides a psychosocial history of how parts of life came to be relegated to a private domain as part of the same process that generated a self-consciousness that stands in sharp contrast to an outer, social world.[7] The psycho- and sociogenetic theory he advanced explores the relationship between being an individual and having a private sphere. Elias depicts social life in the early Middle Ages as one in which there were few functional relationships between people outside of their local community. Although people had reason to fear starvation or slaughter, they had little need to restrain themselves in their expression of their impulses, passions, and emotions. What we think of as inner life, they lived openly. Life was characterized by belligerence, joy in tormenting others, hatred, gaiety – all spontaneously following upon one another. Social customs and sensibilities were radically different. During the early Middle Ages attitudes toward sex were quite different: In order for a marriage to be valid, the bride and the groom, after being disrobed by their attendants, had to be placed naked on the bridal bed together in the presence of witnesses.[8] This practice evidences the degree to which virginity and consummation were key elements in marriage practices.[9] But they also illustrate the extent to which social structure was incorporated into the marital relationship. Marriage as an institution was not an escape from social control.

As political, economic, and social life became more complex, and as social functions became much more differentiated, individuals were compelled to regulate their conduct, checking their impulsive character through a process of internalization of the principles of "correct" conduct – that is, conduct that allows one to carry out one's varied functional relationship, independent of how one is inclined. Society changed its structure in moving from a basically agrarian, socially disassociated mass of small communities to a socially integrated economic and political state. Similarly, the structure of individual consciousness changed from one of impulsive and mercurial behavior patterns to one of habitually internalized restraints that accommodated to the demands of the more interrelated social fabric. The internalization of restraints on natural impulses and bodily functions led to an attitude change. What belonged to the sphere of the instinctive and natural desires was something that had to be removed from the public scene and relegated to a socially hidden dimension of life. If self-control was not adequately displayed, individuals were to experience shame at having their nonsocial self appear in a social context. The domestic setting and one's own private mental world became the only acceptable scenes for the expression of this impulsive and natural self, now banished from the public world. Before this development, there was little or no distinction between the public and private worlds, between the personal and the social worlds, between the internal life and the manifest life.

As the social control mechanisms became internalized, because one's social relationships with others often led to combinations of hostility and dependence, the self experienced itself in a great deal of inner conflict. Powerful elements of self cannot be revealed to the world because they conflict with what people regard as necessary for social interdependence, and because of the powerful influence of socialization mechanisms on our innermost nature. Our very souls become imprinted with repressive codes. The unexpressed part of the self is experienced as the inner or real self, in constant battle with one's social, outer world. Internalized social control mechanisms engender "inner life." Elias's treatment of socialization is reminiscent of Nietzsche's discussion in his *Genealogy of Morals* and of Freud's discussion in *Civilization and Its Discontents*, as comes out clearly in the following passage:

> He is now less a prisoner of his passions than before. But as he is now more tightly bound by his functional dependence on the activities of an ever-larger number of people, he is much more restricted in his conduct, in his chances of directly sat-

isfying his drives and passions. Life becomes in a sense less dangerous, but also less emotional or pleasurable, at least as far as the direct release of pleasure is concerned. And for what is lacking in everyday life a substitute is created in dreams, in books and pictures. . . . Part of the tensions and passions that were earlier directly released in the struggle of man and man must now be worked out within the human being. . . . But the drives, the passionate affects that can no longer directly manifest themselves in relationships *between* people, often struggle no less violently *within* the individual against this supervising part of himself.[10]

The individual only emerges in certain kinds of historical circumstances, because to be an individual *is* to be aware of oneself in conflict with society's norms, internalized so as to give rise to inner conflict. This individual self-awareness finds a need for private spheres and, as a result, reassigns the instinctive and less socialized parts of self to domestic and mental settings.

The history of the self that Elias relates is corroborated by developments in religious institutions. Rather than spontaneously springing forth, the religious orders nurtured and cultivated an inner life among their own members at first and eventually in the community of the faithful at large. Confession of wicked thoughts to their elders on the part of monks was an innovation that introduced introspection. Internalization of conflict emerged from this spiritual process. Silence and meditation were introduced as techniques to focus on spiritual progress and cultivate the inner man.[11]

Though introduced largely as a means of increasing control over people and rooting out heresy, confession, once the exclusive practice of those in religious orders, became a requirement covering everyone Christian. In 1215, the Fourth Lateran Council made private and regular confession compulsory. There were profound consequences of the shift from the public spectacle of penance to the private dialogue between one's soul and one's God.[12] And as the introduction of a money economy at the time gave currency to the notion of earning wealth and thereby improved material and social status, a spiritual metaphor followed in which inner acts earned one a place in the spiritual order. Economic and religious transformations together forged a sense of self that could be set against others in the community.

Writing proved to be advantageous for those who wanted both to administer their property well and leave their heirs material and spiritual capital. One can find evidence in family archives that, after 1350, people organized and classified the various notes containing this material. The introduction of accounting ledgers led to the separate treatment of financial and personal records, including memoirs. These memoirs created a particular opportunity to focus on an intimate self that contrasted with either family ties or religious obligations.[13]

If the self and a sense of intimacy are to evolve from these historical processes, it is not without an extended struggle, a struggle that is far from complete at the point we left it. A discussion of changes in family life that occurred in England between the sixteenth century and the nineteenth can bring us closer to an end that we can recognize.[14]

I begin with two major claims about English family life in the early sixteenth century: First, the nuclear family, husband, wife, and children, did *not* constitute an intimate environment in which participants focused special emotional resources on, and in turn derived special emotional meaning from, their relations with one another; and, second, privacy in one's most important relationships, including one's relationship to oneself, was not an active norm. The development of intimacy and meaning in personal relations and the emergence of privacy norms are correlated with the emergence of the individual as the basic social unit replacing the kin group. The conception of a person as an individual comes only when individuals ask questions about life's meanings and goals and then have the responsibility of finding suitable answers. Individuals are not just entities given naturally in their entirety, but are constructed by their own personal experiences, the associations in which they participate, and the ways in which they resolve conflicts.

A description of the family norms at the turn of the sixteenth century supports my claim that the nuclear family was not an intimate environment:

> In the sixteenth century, and almost certainly for at least a millennium before, the characteristic type, especially among the social elite, was what I have chosen, for lack of a better term, to call the Open Lineage Family, since its two most striking features were its permeability by outside influences, and its members' sense of loyalty to ancestors and to living kin. The principal boundary circumscribed the kin, not its sub-unit, the nuclear family. This was a society where neither individual autonomy nor privacy were respected as desirable ideals. It was generally agreed that the interests of the group, whether that of the kin, the village, or later the state, took priority over the wishes of the individual and the achievement of his particular ends. . . . Conventional wisdom was that happiness could only be anticipated in the next world, not in this, and sex was not a pleasure but a sinful necessity justified only by the need to propagate the race. Individual freedom of choice ought at all times and in all respects to be subordinated to the interests of others, whether lineage, parents, neighbors, kin, church, or state. As for life itself, it was cheap, and death came easily and often. The expectation of life was so low that it was highly imprudent to become too emotionally dependent upon any other human being. Outside court circles, where it flourished, romantic love was in any case regarded by moralists and theologians as a kind of mental illness. . . .
>
> As a result, relations within the nuclear family, between husband and wife, parents and children, were not much closer than those with neighbors, relatives, or with "friends." . . . Marriage was not an intimate association based on personal choice. Among the upper and middling ranks it was primarily a means of tying two kinship groups, of obtaining collective economic advantages and securing useful political alliances. Among peasants, artisans and laborers, it was an economic necessity for partnership and division of labor in the shop or in the field. For both men and women it was the price of economic survival, while for the latter it was the only career available. So far as society was concerned, it was a convenient way of channeling the powerful but potentially disruptive instinct of sexual desire – which it was assumed could be satisfied

by any reasonably presentable member of the opposite sex –
and it made possible the production and rearing of legitimate
children. . . . Nor did most young people resent such a system,
since for them the association in marriage was only one of
many social relationships, and personal accommodation to circumstances, necessity and authority was an ingrained pattern
of behavior.[15]

The picture of social relations that Stone paints is one of
abject material and social conditions, engendering the pathological social alienation we find today plaguing abused and
neglected children.

What is being postulated for the sixteenth and early seventeenth centuries is a society in which a majority of the individuals that composed it found it very difficult to establish
close emotional ties to any other person. Children were neglected, brutally treated, and even killed; adults treated each
other with suspicion and hostility; affect was low and hard to
find. . . .
There seem to have been four causes for the development
of such a culture. The first was the frequency with which
infants at that period were deprived of a single mothering and
nurturing figure to whom they could relate during the first
eighteen months or two years of life. Upper class babies were
mostly taken from their real mothers and put out to wet-nurse.
These nurses were often cruel or neglectful, and they often
ran out of milk, as a result of which the baby had to be passed
from nipple to nipple, from one unloving mother-substitute
to another. . . .[16]

Most men and women of the sixteenth and seventeenth centuries, from all walks of life, to differing degrees, show very
clearly evidence of all the overt symptoms of parental de-
privation.[17]

[These symptoms include:] chronic low grade depression; a
sense of abandonment; a feeling of emptiness; deep dependency needs; an inability to maintain human relationships;
psychotic-like attacks of rage; and a tendency to erect protective defenses against the world, giving a paranoid coloration
to their character. . . .

Many children of all classes suffered the loss by death of one parent or another at an early age.

There was deliberate breaking of the young child's will, first by the harshest physical beatings and later by overwhelming psychological pressures, which was thought to be the key to successful childrearing.[18]

High adult mortality rates . . . severely reduced the companionship element in marriage and increased its purely reproductive and nurturance functions. There was less than a fifty-fifty chance that the husband and wife would remain alive more than a year or two after the departure from the home of the last child, so that friendship was hardly necessary.[19]

In the sixteenth century, however, family relationships were characterized by interchangeability, a lack of individual commitment so that substitution of another wife or another child was easy, and by conformity to external rules of conduct.[20]

Because the struggle to survive took such a high percentage of the individual's resources, and because life was fraught with such material insecurity, there was little opportunity for intimate nurturance. There was just much less of a personal nature to the contribution individuals made to their immediate social environment. To use terminology introduced in Chapter 1, people had roles to play, but no relationships to be part of. Associations were all-encompassing and individuals were dispensable.

Even among the well-to-do, domestic life was diffused through the presence of numerous servants and relatives living in the same quarters as the nuclear family. Strong allegiances to many stand in the way of intense ties to a few. Among the poorer sectors, everyone was crowded into the one or two all-purpose rooms that composed houses. Among the lower classes, economic life was strictly regulated by community decisions to the extent that all aspects of economic planning came under collective control. Because individual marriage plans could also affect who had rights to work the land, economic pressures were put on widows in their choices of whom to remarry. Finally, village life was characterized by intense scrutiny and intrusion into the lives of neighbors.

> Everyone gossiped freely about the most intimate details of domestic relations, and did not hesitate to denounce violations of community norms . . . so that people were constantly testifying in court about the alleged moral peccadilloes of their neighbors.[21]

Initially one might be hard pressed to explain how this is different from what seems common today. Part of the answer lies in the concurrence of the legal and the social sanction that was, but is no longer, the case. Another part lies in the social norms themselves. People today, like people always, are fascinated with intimate details of the lives of others, but unlike the past, an atmosphere of tolerance, even if grudging, pervades our assessment of others' lives. We internalize that many aspects of other people's lives just aren't our business, and this severely limits the social consequences of norm violations. In accord with what was described in the preceding chapter, we appreciate that our basis of relating to people excludes a lot of dimensions of other people's lives, so that the things about them that might interest us do not affect or threaten our relationship to them. In the next chapter, I discuss in detail the interdependence of privacy and gossip.

As outlined in Chapter 1, I differentiate two senses of privacy: one that permits personal expression and one that merely keeps outsiders at bay. In colonial times, however little there was of the latter, there was none of the former. David Flaherty's work on privacy in colonial New England describes a public officer whose role it was to scrutinize and ensure a proper domestic order.[22] There were fewer norms that precluded individuals from gaining access to the lives of others, from making discoveries about people, from revealing publicly what was discovered, and from these discoveries having legal effect. Those norms that did stand in the way of intrusions were not conceived as limitations that respect for privacy demands. Most elements of what we consider a right to personal privacy were not operative in colonial times in the United States or England.

There were no decisions or areas of life deemed so personal that strong public pressures were thought unfitting to bring to bear in order to encourage socially acceptable outcomes. This point is worth illustrating with a number of examples. What to labor at, when to labor, with whom, whom to marry, whether to have children, whom to have in one's house, whom to associate with – none of these areas provided people with socially shielded options. Prying into personal lives to see whether there were infractions of community norms was not just a common pastime but a source of endless complaints to officials aimed at securing compliance. Matters of individual religious faith were characteristically thought open to public exposure and punishable if deviant. Even those who were liberal on this issue thought higher authorities legitimate in punishing for heresy and distinguished themselves by seeking something like probable cause before a person could be held publicly accountable for his or her religious convictions. We have been reminded by constitutional historians that tolerance was the result of a political compromise between intolerant groups who feared for their own security, and not the outcome of a respect for the consciences of others.

It has already been mentioned that preference in marriage partners was subordinated to political and economic concerns of the families or the parties themselves. Calvinists insisted that the potential for a loving relationship between two people was an essential criterion for choosing a marriage partner. Among the motivations for inclusion of this objective was the hope that love between spouses would reduce the amount of adultery. This did not mean that sex between spouses escaped being a fit subject for regulation. Some equated too much pleasure in sex, even with one's own spouse, as similar morally to adultery. One matter on which Calvinists and Catholics were agreed in this period is that not too much intensity should accompany marital intercourse, because, first of all, this diverts one's realization that the purpose of intercourse is largely procreation and, second, intense pleasure from the experience may encourage the parties to seek similar enjoyments outside of the marriage relationship. In fairness, it should be acknowledged that there are still social, religious, and, in many cases, legal regulations of marital, sexual conduct.

In the early part of the eighteenth century, after public concern with fornication as a sin diminished, the principal concern of the community became that of avoiding the financial burdens that children born out of wedlock imposed. One strategy the communities employed was to transport unwed pregnant woman outside of their boundaries and avoid the burden by estranging the woman. Worse still, it was a common practice for midwives to interrogate the expectant unwed mother about the identity of the father *during the agony of labor*, offering her assistance only after she supplied a name. The midwives' oath of 1726 imposed this duty upon them.[23] It would be hard to think of behavior more intrusive into an individual's privacy and intimacy than this. One final example, tame by comparison with the last, relates to a form of entertainment that is still with us. Throughout the middle of the eighteenth century "the monthly periodical *Town and Country Magazine* entertained its readers in each issue with an illustrated account of the irregular sex life of some man of note."[24]

If we think about the locus and desiderata of decision making, the kinds of relationships people had, the sensitivities, the expectations, we get a bleak picture of the level at which privacy functioned as a meaningful moral, legal, or social category.

The history of the legal status of marriage provides some interesting perplexities for someone thinking about the role of privacy and intimacy. Through the Middle Ages the popular, lay view of marriage was that of a personal affair of no concern to political authorities. In the early Middle Ages, it was thought of merely as a private contract between two families regulating property exchange and the financial protection for the wife in case of death or desertion by the husband. It was not until the thirteenth century that the church succeeded in imposing the ideal of monogamous and indissoluble marriage into the law. Still marriage remained, in England at least, a hopelessly confusing affair, with numerous means available for validly marrying and remarrying without questions being asked about prior status. This situation threatened the welfare of noble families, because it gave uncooperative children ways of marrying someone the parents thought would ruin the family's honor or financial and political prospects. So marriage acts were introduced that would nullify marriages of children under twenty-one without the consent of their parents.

Diverse sets of factors contributed to the emergence of the interrelated categories of intimacy, privacy, and individuality within the social fabric: factors that undermined the dominant role of kin groups, increased the significance of the conjugal group, and heightened consciousness of the individual as such. I start with factors that undermined the social importance of the kin group.

First is the ascendancy of the political state. As political institutions afforded individuals greater protection, people became less dependent on their kin groups for security. Urban immigration, impoverishment in the towns, and devastating effects of inflation required a shifting of the burden for the welfare of the sick, the helpless, the aged, and the orphans away from kin groups and to the communities. Also, the growth of the market economy brought into being new economic strata and organization. Prospects arose for earning an income and improving the quality of life by residing in a city. New attitudes toward property developed that allowed for economic rights not tied to social obligation.[25] These factors deprived the kin group of some of its influence and provided individuals some measure of increased independence from its control.

Numerous factors promoted the conjugal family as the central institution in which individuals were to invest meaning and find emotional solace. The conjugal family's significance became heightened as the kin group receded in importance and as individuals came to see themselves as positioned to find meaning in life as a result of choices they made for themselves. Puritanism fostered the notion of marriage as an institution bound by mutual affection, which required allowing some measure of personal choice to persons embarking on marriage and, with it, the eventual recognition of rights of adult children over their own lives.

There were some significant ways in which the decline of Catholic institutions deprived women of some traditional sources of social relationships outside of their marriage. The prospect of emotional and moral support that was available to women in the confessional waned along with the influence of the Catholic church. The career option of entering a nunnery diminished. The decline of the priest and the importance invested in public worship served to shift religious authority to the husbands and in so doing added still further authority to the already unequal balance of power between husbands and wives.[26]

In the economic domain, enclosing of the common fields undermined cooperative village farming and, with it, community control over family decisions. Economic and geographic mobility meant a loosening of the bonds to extrafamilial social and authority structures. Furthermore, the custom of the dowry going to the groom's parents was being replaced by the practice of using the dowry to invest in land to give the new couple heightened economic potential. This empowered the wife, making her a major economic contributor to her own life.

These developments meant that emotional ties with people outside the nuclear family – friends, neighbors, and relatives – were continually being eroded. One's status as a link between past and future generations became an ever smaller part of one's identity.[27] As relationships outside the family became less intense and significant, those within the family became the nearly exclusive focus of one's social resources. A fusing of two types of sexual expression was taking place: that of marital roles for the production of male heirs and that of sexual relationship for love and companionship.

As a result of the changed social, religious, and economic

climate, much more of an individual's identity focused on the nuclear family than earlier, especially for women whose traditional social ties were now proving highly volatile. A woman's future, more than before, was tied to the marriage she made.

The practical difficulties of fusing the romantic and the traditional archetypes into a real life became a new theme in popular literature, and women's fascination with this theme largely accounts for the burgeoning of the novel as a literary form. Domestic life now had enough complexity and texture to be the subject of unlimited depictions.[28]

A great theme of the early novel is that of displacement of the individual upon confronting the impersonal city in which no personal relationships can be taken for granted. In this urban experience, there is no overriding sense of community or common standards to organize the diverse elements of social life. In the anonymity of urban life, one belongs to many social groups, each isolated from the rest, with no overall pattern connecting them together into a consistent whole. It is this pattern that facilitates the emergence of social freedom. This social context leaves a great deficit in the individual's sense of security and understanding. The response to this deficit was to seek what was lost in "the shared intimacies of personal relationships."[29] What we think of as private life was taken to be the answer to this great social and personal problem.

The decline of status as the important social determinant and the rise of economic, social, and geographic mobility meant that one's position in social life was not fixed and that one could occupy different positions or roles. Because what one was in society could change, what one *was* and what one *was socially* represented different facets of a person – just the split needed to give rise to a public sense of a private sphere.[30] This is the phenomenon of value entropy suggested in the preceding chapter.

The nuclear family and the significance of the individual as individual seemed to emerge simultaneously. I have been suggesting that our idea of the individual was not instantiated before this period. And even when we talk about the emergence of the individual, it is important to recognize that what is meant by "individual" is not a being that is socially disengaged, but rather a person who has some say over which associations include her.

One way of describing the emergence of "the individual" to make it seem less paradoxical is to think that what is emerging in the eighteenth century is the significance of the relationships one makes for oneself, and a diminution of those over which one has no control. Ian Watt describes the rise of the novel in this period as the result of a shift in literary and social interest away from coverage of abstract and generic topics and toward individual experience. The individual's private experience – not traditional themes from mythology, history, or legend – then became the terrain to explore.[31]

Lionel Trilling describes the character revolution that is occurring at this period, aware of the sense of paradox occasioned by claims that individuals were not part of the social picture before the middle of the seventeenth century.[32]

The new kind of personality which emerged . . . is what we call an "individual": at a certain point in history man became individual.

Taken in isolation, the statement is absurd. How was a man different from an individual? . . . But certain things he did not have or do until he became an individual. He did not have an awareness of . . . internal space. He did not . . . imagine himself in more than one role, standing outside or above his own personality; he did not suppose that he might be an object of interest to his fellow man not for the reason that he achieved something notable or been witness to great events, but simply because as an individual he was of consequence.[33]

And he begins to use the word "self" not as a mere reflexive or intensive, but as an autonomous noun referring . . . to . . . that which he must cherish for its own sake and show to the world for the sake of good faith. . . . His conception of his private and uniquely interesting individuality, together with his impulse to reveal his self, to demonstrate that in it which is to be advanced and trusted, are, we may believe, his response to the newly available sense of an audience, of that public which society created.[34]

For this kind of change in conception to occur, the hierarchical arrangement of domains of life must have given way to a less well ordered organization of relationships that could now compete with one another. As the various domains of life acquired independent meaning and took on value in and of themselves, individuals had to make decisions, in part based on how the competing domains of life struck them as important.

Other factors principally reoriented the individual's conception of himself in relationship to various authorities, including that of the kin group. To begin with, the Reformation undermined the unity of Christendom in a way that left individuals with options and an awareness of the fallibility of every institution that professes to be authoritative. Appreciating just how much was lost through this religious challenge may, ironically, account for the fanaticism so many resorted to in an effort to assure themselves that an objective, all-embracing order was really still in effect.[35] Even before the Reformation, the Inquisition in Spain and Portugal necessitated the awareness of individual responsibility for religious identification in Jews and Moslems forced to convert or be expelled, and in the "Christian" descendants of these converts who maintained awareness of, and identification with, their family's history.[36]

Generally, the Puritan emphasis on the dignity of labor led to a conflation of religious and material values. Attributing great spiritual value to performance of daily tasks promoted the attitude that success in mastering the environment represented obedience to God's expectations of us.[37]

An intense interest in introspection was implicit in the Puritan practice of self-examination and self-discipline. Spiritual introspection was continually monitored to reveal one's "place in the divine plot of election and reprobation."[38]

Literacy provided people with a new kind of private experience for discovering and considering ideas without confronting direct social pressure. Puritanism also emphasized the importance of individual conscience and of private prayer. After a reign of fanaticism imposed by the Calvinists, English society reacted with a new appreciation for tolerance of individual idiosyncrasies.

Scientific, medical, and technological developments also fostered the notion that individuals are in control of their own fate and can benefit by actively seeking to promote their own well-being. Poverty, misery, and disease were no longer conditions that had to be confronted passively. The religious and scientific developments put more significance into the quality of one's earthly existence and relationships. These factors contributed to the abandonment of the principle of human interchangeability. An appreciation for the uniqueness of each person replaced fungibility of persons.

What are the connections between according individual experience a sense of dignity and the evolution of a sense of privacy as an operative social category? It is one thing to acknowledge that the experience of a person is private in the sense that it is hers and no one else's, and another to say that certain elements of the individual's experience should be protected from social scrutiny and regulation. Without being able to offer a satisfactory answer at the present, we can suggest a number of relevant factors that constitute part of an account.

With the distinction between social role and person, some value is to be accorded the latter independent of the former. This underlying stratum, the so-called real person, is seen as the ultimate moral unit, deserving of protection and respect in its own right, and not just because of the functional role it occupies. Its source of dignity is detachable from the specific social fields it occupies. Because it is not dependent on any particular context for its value, it implicitly imposes a limit on what can be done to beings to achieve any particular social objective. It is capable of standing in opposition to society or taking a critical attitude toward it. This perspective makes it a resource for reform, even if an unwelcome one at the time. This self requires a space of its own to be what it is. This space is the private world.

My description here of the self or inner person is meta-physically loaded. Though it is tempting to see the self as a substratum, divorced from each of its public manifestations, its conditions of identity need not really require it to function as the authentic actor behind the social roles. It would be enough to posit resources to the self that can be derived from any of the particular roles it plays.

Social life, as we saw, changed from one of unbounded social involvement and diffuse, traditionally determined relationships organized within a value hierarchy to one of social indifference and highly focused, individually determined relationships unorganized by any overarching value. What became most meaningful to the individual was not something that resulted from what was, or even in principle could be, shared by all, but something peculiar to oneself. As social bonds and interdependency with one's neighbors weakened, their claim to any authoritative say over the entire range of a person's affairs became attenuated. The emergence of limited functional relationships between people meant that most of a person's life would be of limited relevance to most others, generating tolerance for what was out of immediate focus. Intrusion into these other domains or roles would threaten the functional relationships that made people economically replaceable in the larger scheme of things. In this more modern scheme of things, there was no authoritative superstructure to put competing roles and allegiances into a coherent whole. Values conflicted and individuals had to live with this complexity, making the requisite choices. Disappointing one set of expectations or one role relationship would not divest the individual of possibilities in other role relationships in which he could dedicate his efforts to find meaning. Human nature was no longer a universal pattern imprinted on each soul, reflecting a preestablished harmony. Rather, nature individuated itself in the case of each person. Fulfilling this distinctive nature, not human nature in general, became each person's trust.[39]

Whereas people were replaceable on the economic and social level, at the domestic level individuals were anything but replaceable – a significant change over family structure in the sixteenth and previous centuries.

The point of the historical narrative has been to show that particular conditions are met before one is likely to find social sensitivity to spheres and protection from public scrutiny and regulation. We can ask whether before these conditions are met, individuals do not, or may not, feel somehow violated by scrutiny and control over parts of their lives that social norms do not protect. As already intimated, there are numerous instances in which people violently protested or in other ways subverted their parents' choice of a marriage partner despite the fact that there was no recognized social norm that could provide a rationale for doing so. What is surprising to us is the extent to which people did not rebel and the extent to which they must have thought very differently about themselves and what is valuable or important in a well-structured life.

In this chapter, I have looked to social structure to reflect moral qualities of a person's soul. Some would find this approach discomforting, because it suggests that we can legitimize harsh treatment of individuals just by structuring social institutions in inhumane ways. Slaveholders and concentration camp operators can point to the social structure and say, this is how these people live so this is what these people are.

A response to this challenge could point to the shift in theory from the historical claim to the critical response. In the historical account, I do not claim that people generated the social structure to vindicate their preferred picture of people, however arrived at. I claim that social structure, and not theorists, determined aspects of moral personality. Social structure did not determine that there would be a class of slaves in the United States from the earliest period. Social structure did not determine that there should be a genocidal policy throughout Europe. These were deliberate policies that were debatable in principle within the cultural contexts within which they arose. The same potential for debate could not be credited to much of the period we reviewed.

Chapter 8

Privacy and gossip

We humanize what is going on in the world and in ourselves only by speaking of it, and in the course of speaking of it we learn to be human. (Hannah Arendt)[1]

There is a puzzle connected with my treatment of privacy that I feel obliged to explore. In the process of exploring the puzzle, we shall have an opportunity to see how privacy interacts with another social category, though one that seems to be at cross-purposes with privacy. I have been arguing that privacy, in one of its important and characteristic roles, insulates people from inappropriate manifestations of social pressure. (Whether a manifestation of social pressure is "inappropriate" is socially and historically variable.) Gossip involves bothering with parts of a person's life that are characteristically none of one's business and introduces an indirect form of social pressure that privacy norms would seem designed to exclude. In contrast to violations of privacy, gossip, though not directed to the individual discussed, does precisely what it would be rude to do directly to the person: discuss what is none of someone's business. Furthermore, gossip gives informational access to an individual in apparent violation of that individual's private domain. In a culture where people know that others gossip, the very social pressure from which we think it is privacy's role to insulate a person is unleashed, though in an attenuated form.

In this chapter, I take some steps toward understanding the apparent conflict between the role of privacy and the role

136

of gossip. The apparent conflict is located in the exclusion in the case of privacy norms, on the one hand, and the invitation in the case of gossip norms, on the other, to concern oneself with what is another person's business. What I would like to show is that despite this apparent conflict, gossip presupposes privacy norms and in so doing works together with privacy norms to protect individuals from overreaching social control. Privacy and gossip norms work together to modulate the amount and type of social pressure available to control behavior.

Discussing gossip in connection with privacy will help us emphasize two features of privacy that it is important to acknowledge: (1) Privacy is part of a historically conditioned, intricate normative matrix with interdependent practices; it is best understood when viewed contextually interacting with other practices in shaping behavior rather than as an independent principle that either succumbs to or overrides other considerations. Seeing privacy in this way, we appreciate that it is central to social life and not a principle that stands in opposition to it. (2) Private behavior and behavior in private contexts, even when most liberated and expressive, is subject to an array of social norms and controls.

The discussion that follows involves first a review discussion of privacy. Privacy, as indicated in Chapter 1, is a fluid and dynamic concept, and clarification is needed to focus on the sense privacy has that is germane to resolving the prima facie conflict between privacy and gossip norms. Next is a discussion of gossip that reviews some of the social science literature that illuminates the virtues of a social practice usually considered a vice. These two discussions are then used to show how the apparent conflict between gossip and privacy norms is only a superficial appearance.

PRIVACY

Forms of control can be inappropriate because the costs of control are too high even though the directions or objectives of the control are in themselves desirable. Also, forms of control can be inappropriate because the direction of the control is wrongful in the first place. An example of the first would be universal use of monitors in the home designed to detect child abuse. An example of the second would be monitors in the home to ensure particular forms of religious observance.

It is impolite for me to say to a work associate who is not a friend, for instance, that she should lose weight or restrict her dating of men. These are matters about which we would say that they are none of my business. What makes these matters – how heavy the colleague is, or how many simultaneous romantic relationships she maintains – none of my business is that according to our cultural rules she *should* not have to deal with the explicit and typically critical discussion of these aspects of her life by me when they are not germane to our work relationship. She is not answerable to me for these aspects of her life. These parts of her life are not germane to our relationship as co-workers.

According to these same social norms, there are parts of every person's life others in general should not have access to without having the consent of the individual concerned or without there being a relationship in place that warrants or legitimizes such discussion. In contrast to a person's co-worker, a person's physician, responsible for advising her on health matters, may and should discuss weight with her. Her close friends, able to judge whether discussion or advice would be constructive, potentially may also raise these topics with her.

Complete strangers, such as people she casually talks with on the ski lift or seatmates on a train trip, in contrast to a co-worker, just because they play such an insignificant role in her everyday life, might get away with intimate discussion without violating our social norms. This is because social pressure from a stranger counts less than pressure from people with whom she has some significant connection and to whom she is potentially vulnerable.

To sharpen our intuitions, let us introduce a line of reasoning that seems oblivious to a distinction evident in the difference between private and public communication. At issue in *The Florida Star v. B.J.F.*, a case that went before the U.S. Supreme Court in 1989, was the press's freedom to publish the name of a rape victim when a state statute explicitly prohibited publication of the names of victims of sexual offenses.[2] The statute at issue states:

> No person shall print, publish, or broadcast, or cause or allow to be printed, published, or broadcast, in any instrument of mass communication the name, address, or other identifying fact or information of the victim of any sexual offense within this chapter.

Because freedom of the press was at issue, the Court demanded that high standards be met in justifying the prohibition. The Court's majority at one point asks how the rape victim's privacy can be protected by a law that restricts only media of mass communication from disseminating information that identifies the victim.

Developing the point of this question in a concurring opinion, Justice Scalia suggests that the harm to the victim is actually greater when communicated informally to people who know the victim than when communicated in mass media to people who do not know the victim. Scalia reasons that because the law designed to protect the victim does not extend to private communication, it cannot be seen as part of a reasonable effort to protect the victim. On account of this failing, the law restricting the press has not met the high standards required of a law that abridges speech and communication.

Of course, what is legally at issue in this case is what is constitutional. Evidently a majority of the justices held that whatever we believe about the difference between private communication and mass communication, there is no constitutional basis for such a demarcation. I am not much interested in that question of constitutional justification but, rather, in the privacy issues raised by the points just cited. Why is it that our privacy norms permit much to be said between people privately that is not allowable publicly? Why do we think that private communication of personal facts is more respectful of a person's privacy than public disclosure, particularly in light of our gossip norms that seem to permit broad exposure of private facts?

In 1991 the exposure of the name of, and intimate details about, the woman who alleges that one of the Kennedys raped her focused a great deal of public attention on questions of journalistic ethics and social attitudes. The *New York Times* defended its detailed account of the complainant's life by saying that she was already exposed nationally by the coverage of other mass media reports, so therefore the *Times* was not responsible for exposing her. What the *Times* did not acknowledge is that even within the mass media, there is a difference between what appears in a paper like the *National Enquirer*, or the *Tattler*, on the one hand, and what appears in a paper like the *Times*, on the other. The *National Enquirer* represents coverage of stories that violate social norms about what it is appropriate to discuss publicly; the *Times* represents what it is fitting to discuss publicly. Many regard the revelations as appearing in the *Times* as undercutting norms of decency and privacy, contributing to their deterioration. Thus we can observe differences even among printed media in terms of their impact on legitimizing boundary crossings.

One might be at first tempted to say that our social norms do apply to private disclosure as much as to public or mass disclosure, but we recognize that public communication is both more easily enforceable as well as enforceable with fewer associated costs than is private communication. One should concede that it is easier and less intrusive of individual lives to enforce restrictions on mass communication than on backyard conversations. One should concede that costs associated with state monitoring of private conversations would be universally regarded as unacceptable to all but totalitarians. The problem is that these concessions have little to do with the major issue of whether privacy norms or the indicated role of privacy is violated by norms related to gossip. We should recognize that we regard public disclosure of some facts as wrong because violative of a person's privacy while at the same time we regard nothing wrong with non-public disclosure of these same facts.

Here it is helpful to note that reference to the public–private distinction is not especially edifying for the issue we are discussing.[3] There are many private realms; disclosures made in some private settings seem consistent with privacy norms, whereas disclosures in other private settings are inconsistent with these same norms. If I say to you, someone I know only casually, out of earshot of anyone else, "You should lose weight," there is a sense in which this is not public communication. Others in general have no access to this criticism. This is very different from putting an ad in a personals column indicating my thoughts both to my subject and the rest of the interested world. Alternatively, if I say to my local lodge, whose members are sworn to secrecy, what I think about your shape or romantic habits, this communication should be considered private and not public for our purposes. What would be public disclosure would typically involve a communicative act normatively open to (nearly) anyone.

Similarly, there are legal proceedings, like family court hearings, in which further communication of information disclosed is prohibited, but where much that is intimate and personal is exposed to strangers acting in official capacities who have no stake in the outcome. Here an innermost sphere is exposed to a wider audience but is nevertheless restricted once so exposed. For these situations, contrasting levels of privacy seems more fitting a measure than contrasting the private with the public.

Even talk about restricted audiences is not part of any strict definition of what counts as private and what as public. It just suggests that for some purposes the disclosure of information to groups, even large groups, might still be considered private provided still other groups are excluded.

It is important to appreciate how fluid and relative the private–public distinction really is. A person can be active in the gay pride movement in San Francisco but be private about her sexual preference vis-à-vis her family in Detroit.[4] A person may be highly visible to other gays at the gay bar but discreet about sexual orientation at the workplace. Surely the streets and newspapers of San Francisco are public places as are the gay bars. Does appearing in some public settings as a gay activist mean that the person concerned has waived her rights to civil inattention, to feeling violated if confronted in another setting? As in the *Florida Star* case, First Amendment law and social understanding of civility clash in delineating what are appropriate subjects and settings for public exposure.[5]

Another distinction that can be usefully interjected here is that between normative and descriptive privacy.[6] The disclosure of a rape victim's name to a public at large does not make the information itself less private in a normative sense, though it does in a descriptive sense. Even if the law requires public disclosure of rape victims' names, so long as we have social norms that understandably adjudge such disclosure as troublesome, we can continue to regard such information as (normatively) private, however widely and legally disseminated. For instance, even if rape victims are not treated as guilty for acting provocatively, or for not resisting enough, and even if it helps to bring public attention to the plight of rape victims to publicize them as identifiable people, there is something intrusive about, and thus there is a cost to, publicizing their names. People who have been raped, like people who have accidentally killed someone or who have lost a loved one, face emotional trauma, and are shrouded by society with a varying set of protective norms within which to manage the trauma.

I began this chapter with the claim that privacy protects people from intrusions into domains of life that are not appropriate realms for some others to confront a person with. To help appreciate this role of privacy, it is useful to recall our discussion in Chapter 1 about two sorts of privacy norms not usually distinguished.

Privacy norms can be part of social control strategies or can enable individuals and groups scope within which to create their own norms. Although both norms shield behavior from some sources of monitoring, the shield may act to restrict rather than liberate behavior. For instance, the privacy accorded parents to raise children may be thought necessary to make children fit some rigid mold, or may be accorded to encourage creativity in the child and her relationships with parents. The first sort of norm does not protect individual expression or place limitations on social regimentation. One and the same privacy norm may at one time be very controlling and at another period allow for individual expression and flexibility.

The privacy norms that promote self-expression are those that involve people in creative roles, and were categorized as norms involving *expressive roles.* What we identified as significant about such norms was their facilitation of deeper and more variable relationships. Notions of privacy and intimacy are suggestive of this possibility. Expressive-role privacy norms enhance prospects for relational ties in which people, within a domain, erase some of the boundaries that separate them from others. Privacy norms, particularly of the expressive-norm sort, can be judged important because of the dimensions of self, both relational and individualistic, that people can generate in supportive social contexts. Because behavior is expressive of the self, it tends to evoke and engage what becomes for them their deepest commitments.

In emphasizing relational dimensions of privacy, I do not want to be taken as denying that privacy is critical to individual creativity.[7] I wish rather to make our understanding of privacy's role more attuned to a dimension typically missed. It is this exclusion of relational dimensions to privacy that is responsible for much of the debate over whether practices like abortion, birth control, and homosexual sex are misleadingly presented as privacy issues and would be more accurately described as autonomy issues.

PRIVACY AND MASS COMMUNICATION

Returning to a case of rape, it would be easy to show some reasons for maintaining different attitudes toward public and private disclosure. If I know that a friend has been raped, I might tell other people who could be sources of support to this person. Mass communication media would result in notifying these same people of the victim's need for assistance, but it would simultaneously notify people who could not be expected to extend support. Indeed, as in the case of *Florida Star v. B.J.F.* mentioned earlier, the rape victim began receiving calls threatening further sexual violence. Besides this, there typically would be plenty of people she does know whom she would not like to have access to this information about her. For instance, a middle-school teacher might well hope that her students are not privy to this information.

This is not to suggest that all gossip is designed to help victims by selectively directing resources to those in need. Presumably only a small percentage of gossip is so directed. In fact, we would probably not regard revelations so directed as gossip in the first place. (Gossip at least should seem idle.) But helping those we know who are in need is an important function of social being, and were privacy norms to really preclude all dissemination, there would be loss of such prospects of expression of support for those in need.

In an essay I published some years ago,[8] I drew attention to an aspect of sharing information about oneself that is germane here. Information that is very emotionally charged for an individual, information that makes or shows an individual particularly vulnerable, is experienced as violating one's innermost self if treated as commonplace. I used the analogy of a sacred object. It is identified as sacred only if understood as something to be treated in a special way.

Reflections like this help us see some difference between the effects of private and mass communication. But the difference is insufficient to bring us to a realistic view of gossip. For gossip is not restricted by norms of privacy or any other relevant norms to pieces of information and situations that treat people as sacred, let alone vulnerable. For instance, if I find out that there is trouble in a relationship between people I do not care for, I do not feel constrained only to convey this to people who will show them support. I might more likely convey this to people who would take some

delight in hearing about other people's, particularly enemies', troubles. If I convey this in the manner suggested, I
do not feel like a social norm violator. (Saints, looking to
different norms, might well regard such communication as
wrong.)

When my mother calls me and tells me about the private
lives of her neighbors, people I knew growing up, I do not
feel that she violates their privacy even though I am neither
situated nor motivated to help them. Nor would the neighbors think my mother should not say such things to me, even
if they would prefer that I not know. I think we all fully
expect to be discussed by others who know us, with no sense
of impropriety. We might think our friends in whom we
confided should hold confidences. But this is different from
thinking that people in whom we have not confided are
restricted in their range of interests in our lives.

Thus, those of us who think that privacy norms are important, even in private life, have to address the question of
how gossip fits into this picture. Maybe privacy as a normative institution is restricted to instruments of mass communication.

THE ROLE OF GOSSIP

Let us shift our attention to gossip. Gossip can be about
almost anything. As Max Gluckman pointed out in one of
the early discussions of gossip,[9] the practice is highly organized by principles of social inclusion and exclusion. Social
cohesion, social identity, social norms, social pressure – these
dynamic factors of social life are all maintained and managed
through the agency of gossip rules.

We reveal the spheres we share with people through the
domains of gossip we exchange with them. To this extent,
gossip is like a special interest newspaper, a public medium. People are sorted into a variety of associations with other people and assume roles or confirm status within these
associations by the sorts of gossip they can competently
manage.

Gossip in some sense is like a secret too, often used to modulate and measure whom we are close to and where our loyalties lie. Gossip spread beyond certain bounds violates important norms. To this extent, gossip is unlike a public medium. Gossip is carefully regulated in its expression and thus not fit for certain public uses.

Unlike a public medium, gossip is informal in the sense that the standards of evidence need not be very high. Although standards are imposed for breaches of whatever rules apply to gossiping under a variety of situations, these standards are socially enforced and to that extent do not precipitate formal sanctions.

As norm-governed behavior, gossip is structured and strictured by norms. People can go too far, or not far enough, vis-à-vis playing by the rules of the game. Several of the standard treatments of gossip focus on its positive contribution to social association and norm maintenance.[10] As Gluckman put the point, people who gossip may be idle, but gossip itself is anything but idle. It is a primary means of maintaining and reinforcing social norms; it is a primary means of holding those in high status to the same standards that govern those not so situated. And it is a way of providing people with information about the social world, revealing both the norms and the extent of noncompliance.

Gossip is also a way of providing people with a sense of what is public and what is not without exposing people to either public ridicule or direct and explicit pressure. Knowing that certain matters are discussed behind people's backs provides one with an incentive not to engage in that behavior, although one also knows that one will not be confronted by most others about the transgression. So long as information remains in the realm of gossip and not treated as public information, the pressure will be attenuated in this way. One will not be accountable to those who know of one's behavior. Still, one knows that others are forming judgments of one based on this information.

What differentiates gossip from news, social news? There is much that we gossip about that we would not think right

146

to reveal "publicly." We may gossip about things we may not publicize, meaning by "publicize" unrestrictedly broadcast to the world at large.

Because we live in a large society with too many people to communicate or gossip with directly, there is in fact a distinction between gossip and publication of news in terms of the scope of people addressed by an act or series of acts of communication. But this is not the key to the difference, or not the only key. For in a smaller community, we could have the same number of people informed by both services: gossip, newspapers. Let me reiterate Gluckman's point that within the gossip norms themselves, there are boundaries that should not be transgressed, information that should not be conveyed.

We surely invade a colleague's privacy if we announce at a meeting that she and our secretary are having an affair. Norms of privacy make this sort of disclosure unconscionable. Norms of privacy, however, do not make it seem as serious, or a serious breach at all, if we simply privately relate the same information to each person in the department, assuming the department is tiny to small. It could even be critical to inform members of the department of this relationship were there a good chance that colleagues unaware of the relationship would end up saying things to the secretary that presuppose emotional distance between him and the colleague.[11] There would, however, be a serious breach if the information were conveyed to someone who would act on it, personally or professionally, to the detriment of the colleague or the secretary.

Thus what we mean by privacy, or invading a person's privacy, is not the fact of disclosing the personal information to a variety of people without the consent of the object of discourse. Rather, the notion of invading a person's privacy by revealing information typically focuses on the means by which the private information is acquired. If someone innocently comes to possess intimate information about another, revealing this information to others in many contexts does not count as an invasion of privacy, although it does lessen the person's privacy and may involve a breach of good taste. Before going on with this, though, a qualification is in order.

Of course there are things one person is entrusted with by another not to reveal, and if this entrusted person reveals, publicly or privately, the information, that is treated as an intrusion into one's privacy and as such presumptively a betrayal. (I say presumptively because it is possible that the revelation is justified by various other considerations.) Other times, even if another individual does not entrust one with information, one may be trusted by the other not to harm her interests, because of the relationship. I do not want to address these sorts of cases here, in part because probably the vast majority of gossip is conveyed by people who have not betrayed a trust in passing on information to the recipient. Still, the fact remains that we think in many such cases that public disclosure of the facts constitutes a wrong, but that back-fence conversation about the same material is no wrong.

I believe I can explain why this is so, in a way that parallels our earlier observations about the *Times* and the *National Enquirer*. Publication of information, at least in some authoritative settings, allows for unrestricted discussion, and allows holding someone answerable for the behavior described. Gossip, even if just as widely disseminated, does not directly affect the public face of the individual. Social norms still preclude acting on the information derived from gossip, especially if this involves holding a person answerable for the behavior.

GOSSIP PRESUPPOSES PRIVACY NORMS

I think this shows that characterizations of privacy as revelation as such are incomplete or misleading. We must differentiate dissemination from publication. Publication means dissemination plus something else. This something else is the conversion of a matter that is personal into a matter that is open or acknowledged as a public fact.

A public fact itself is something established by norms. Just because something happens in public does not mean it becomes a public fact. The Central Park rape occurred April 19, 1989, in public, as did the trial of the accused in that rape, but the victim maintained a measure of privacy as to her identity. In less dramatic cases, the notion of civil inattention directs us to the same realization. We protect the dignity and public persona of a person by not discussing or publicly acknowledging, in a way unconstrained by certain considerations, what is apparent to all. A colleague's ex-wife, for instance, can be heard down the hall hollering at him that he is not paying child support and is a rotten father. Everyone hears this. It is still not a matter for open discussion. People discuss it outside the presence of the colleague. But deference toward the colleague precludes us from acknowledging our awareness of this incident and treating the incident as a public fact. Even publication of something in the *National Enquirer* does not necessarily convert information from private to public, in a normative sense.

Gossip as a social practice is private communication in the sense that it is not addressed to an unrestricted audience. To this extent, privacy and gossip converge in strictures on disclosure.

Gossip permits a person to maintain a public face despite everyone's knowing something that might undermine this presentation but is derived from a different sphere of life. The person presents himself as professionally responsible and emotionally collected despite being domestically irresponsible and badly shaken by events. Is this hypocrisy that we can afford to tolerate? Wouldn't it be better for this to be exposed? Wouldn't we understand more about people and perhaps enable people to realize more about what they share with others without the restrictions on open or unrestricted disclosure, especially of what is known anyway?

Rules governing gossip, like rules governing privacy, are designed to respect different spheres of life, according them each an autonomy. There is a presumption that what a person does in one domain is functionally irrelevant to what she does in another domain. This restriction in use of information is respected so long as from a social perspective the amount of social control available within the domain is adequate to maintain the practice. Were forms of local pressure inadequate and if the practice or domain is treated as important enough, then limited sorts of publication, domain crossing, are permitted or arguably permissible.

It seems as if privacy norms and gossip norms allow us to have it both ways. Gossip norms permit or advance social knowledge and other ends served by gossip norms, and they allow the person concerned insulation as an agent from the direct and decontextualized social pressure of complying with social norms that result from accountability to those with no role within the domain of behavior. Privacy norms, in turn, define the presumptive boundaries within which it is permissible to apply direct social pressure of accountability and threaten social disgrace. We need privacy to understand and engage in gossip because we need the domains of life demarcated to gossip properly. So rather than privacy and gossip working at cross-purposes, we see that privacy norms are a precondition of gossip norms.

We convey information about individuals when we gossip, but not publicly. We thereby combine what might seem like the benefits of both strategies: The person is left to maintain his various functional relationships and private resources; other people are informed about norm deviation, and thereby the norm transgressed is reinforced, reaffirmed community-wide. And other people can also continue to relate to the individual without raising the specter of what might be a highly charged emotional unraveling. The fact that this is not open to public discourse means the individual maintains control over what he will have to address, answer for. Thereby the individual retains resources for managing his own psychic economy.

Chapter 9

Privacy and spheres of life

In this chapter, I introduce the notion of a 'sphere of life' as a category of moral analysis, particularly helpful in thinking about privacy. The notion is implicit in what we have already covered. To prepare for this, some review is in order. In Chapter 1, we saw several aspects of personality and intimacy that are protected by institutions and practices of privacy. These include the following: (1) insulation of personal relationships from accountability for social or global ends and norms, (2) protection of individuals from unconditioned exposure of central emotional vulnerabilities, and (3) encouragement of emotional investment in potentially self-expressive roles and relationships.

In Chapter 6, the overall role of privacy was elaborated in social-evolutionary terms. The more vulnerable to extinction one's community, the more extensive will be the range of expected solidarity and interdependence. As expected solidarity and interdependence increase, social pressure increases as well.

As social survival becomes secure, and as flourishing becomes feasible, tolerance for deliberate change increases and, with it, reliance on individual innovation. Functionally focused associations emerge and replace all-embracing associative communities. Individuals become less dependent on the all-embracing community and more dependent on clusters of functionally focused associations. This change deracinates the prospect of monolithic social hegemony.

Individuals experience variable, and to some extent voluntary, sets of involvements that collectively satisfy personal and group needs. Freedom of association evolves as centralized authority degenerates. Individuals as well as groups are liberated to pursue local goals not entirely structured by global community goals. In place of a single, traditional authority that speaks for the entire community, distributed authorities speak for the locally relevant interests that various associations promote. On this basis, we located social freedom, a large element in human freedom, in freedom of association. I argued that a person's effectiveness as a social agent depends on participation in groups. These groups are critical in protecting individuals from many forms of power and social control, but the effectiveness of these groups depends on their own capacity to influence individual members. Because these groups typically do not have alternative means at their disposal, they employ dynamics of social pressure to encourage loyalty and cohesion. I identify social oppression with inappropriate or overbearing pressure to abide by the principles of a group or, at times, in exclusion from socially important groups where there are not available alternative routes to the ends served by the exclusive group.

As monolithic social authority diminishes, so does the prospect of a unified system of rules and principles that covers all domains of life. (I labeled this phenomenon "value entropy.") This suggests that a proper moral understanding will reflect, rather than obscure, the value structure implicit in everyday life. This value structure includes respect for the integrity of groups as well as individuals and includes allowance for localized ends that do not serve, or to some extent disserve, social purposes. It embraces context- or practice-specific rules of evaluation. In sum, it embraces the integrity of different spheres of life, especially when these spheres are not compressible into a monolithic vision everyone can be expected to share and on which social survival is dependent. Thus, as I elaborated in Chapters 3, 4, and 5, traditional moral theory, which so characteristically seeks such a vision, misrepresents something fundamental about modern moral and social experience. Nevertheless, when socially critical ends are at stake, forms of control of individuals or groups become legitimate that would be illegitimate in pursuit of less urgent goals.

What emerged through the discussion is that the common dichotomy between individuals and the state or society masks something important and thereby misdirects our analysis of social agency. We are free from the power of *the* state or *the* society, not when we judge and act without reference to the attitudes of others as Mill and those in his tradition advocate, but when we have available diverse social groups to which we can adhere and contribute, and from which we can garner support. We exercise our freedom not by our indifference to others' goals and attitudes, but by belonging and participating in various associations. By and large, we express ourselves as effective agents of social change through such associations. One important way we have of limiting the authority of *the* state and of *the* society is through embracing the authority and respecting the integrity of diverse social unions. When this diversity is unavailable or inaccessible to some, prospects for social freedom are diminished for them. Because the individual is the locus of choice, in a sense, this is individualism. But that label belies or obscures the essentially relational, contextualized connections that enable the individual to be free in *both* the negative and positive senses. Diverse associations enable people to be *free* from the control of others because of two factors: Any one association is just one of several dissociated associations to which we belong and through which we achieve ends important to our lives, and thus our vulnerability to any one set of associative ties is limited. Many of our associative ties represent merely one route for achieving roughly similar ends. Diverse associations also enable us to be free *to* become effective social agents. Were we to think about ourselves as one person against a society uniform in every attitude, our prospect for social impact would be negligible. But that is not the profile of a person's relationship to society. Although there are significant social power differentials, there are generally associative options available to people to further ends deemed important by them that can be pursued in a context of social support.

An appreciation of the crushing potential organized social forces have is easily illustrated. Consider the difficulties homosexuals have, not just in revealing themselves publicly as homosexuals but even in accepting homosexuality in themselves. Outside of the homosexual communities themselves, much of the social world is antagonistic at best. The consequences for psychic peace on the part of homosexuals is devastating. This, not surprisingly, is what it is meant to be. It is society's message to those tempted to skirt its deeply felt norms. Few can live in the context of such contempt and hostility without psychic wounds. Minority populations face the same problems of self-respect in being noticeably different, physically and culturally.

To counter this oppression to even some extent, two strategies are necessary. One is that there be communities that support the validity of homosexual (or ethnically distinctive) existence. These communities too must impose some measure of conformity to be effective. After all, the victims of the oppression have also internalized the dominant values that plague them. Those in out-groups are fated to a split consciousness.[1] The enemy lies within as well as outside the agent.

The second is that privacy between communities be respected. In suggesting this we revert to our appreciation that there is not just one public and one private domain, but many of each. Segregation of role is critical. Information exposed to one community should be private relative to another.

Let me illustrate the significance of this point about the role of the segregation of spheres of life. Oliver Sipple, a Vietnam War veteran, was active in the gay rights movement in the 1970s in San Francisco. His family, living in Detroit, knew nothing of his sexual orientation. In 1975, Sipple was propelled to the status of a hero by knocking the revolver out of the hand of Sara Moore after it was aimed and fired once at President Gerald Ford.

Major newspapers revealed that Sipple was actively gay

and part of the gay rights movement. This revelation brought about estrangement from his family, and that in turn exacerbated serious psychological and social problems. Sipple committed suicide ten years after he had saved the president's life.[2]

One might ask what was the point of the newspaper revelations that Sipple is gay in a story about his heroism. Some gay activists argue that only through such revelations will we ever be able to normalize being gay. Journalists will argue that because Sipple's heroism made him a figure of public interest, the revelation of personal details was both legal and helpful to the public in getting a fuller picture of the person. Both approaches avoid focusing on the individual costs suffered in pursuit of the ends they espouse. To the activists, we could respond that there are enough gay people who are open about this fact of their lives so that their goal can be accomplished without imposing sacrifices. To the journalist we could respond that maybe this fuller picture is not worth its costs. No public decision was pending in which Sipple's sexual orientation figured. Indeed, the only understanding we might derive from the case is the potentially disastrous consequence of such public revelations, even of public facts, across domains of life.

Although the distinction between the public and the private is surely indispensable, an analysis in terms of spheres of life can prove illuminating. As we just saw, the revelation of a public fact (Sipple's gay activism in San Francisco) in one setting to a different setting (news about the person who saved the president's life available in Detroit) contributed to Sipple's fate. If we feel that Sipple was somehow violated in the news coverage, it cannot be because a private fact was revealed about him. Political activism, like appearance at a gay bar, is not a private act (or behavior), though it does suggest something about private dimensions of a person's life. I want to explore in this and the next chapter the notion that what is critical in this case and in what we think of as protecting privacy generally is appreciating that different domains of life deserve protection from various kinds of intrusion. When you protect a domain from certain kinds of intrusion, you are necessarily excluding some from having an influence. But it is misleading to think that because some are excluded, the exclusion protects a person as such and not a social relationship or association, and not a public association.

In Chapter 1, I suggested that the fact that we seek protection from state and social intrusion or control is not necessarily best understood in terms of the notion of autonomy, as opposed to privacy. The reason is that both the means of protection and the point of being protected in many instances are the same – the desire to relate to people in important ways. Whereas privacy suggests involvement and intimacy, autonomy suggests isolation. That is to say, privacy has two aspects: "privacy from" and "privacy for." The "privacy from" aspect suggests restrictions on others' access to a person. But typically there is this other dimension to the concept, the "privacy for" dimension. For instance, I am accorded privacy from most others vis-à-vis my domestic life so that I may form deep and special relationships with family or friends. Without this end in view, the contours of the privacy accorded domestic life would be very different.[3] Characteristic defenses of privacy as well as characteristic associations with what we mean by privacy suggest interpersonal or even social affairs. Even the privacy associated with freedom of thought and conscience has strong associationalist aspects, involving access to others' ideas and influences. Because of these connotations, we misrepresent issues like abortion and birth control as antiassociational or asocial, rather than as deeply associational, when we categorize the issue in autonomy terms rather than in privacy terms. Rights to birth control and abortion are aspects of relating to another intimately, and not characteristically a means of alienating oneself from all others. By conceiving freedom in associational terms, we help to emphasize the social aspects of freedom. By connecting social control with associational effectiveness we establish or help make more salient the connecting, rather than the conflicting, features of the categories: freedom, control, agency, and privacy.

In the next chapter, I illustrate the fit of decentralized norms to life and the associational basis of decision making, at least as depicted in Henry James's novels and stories. In that analysis, several observations about the scope and role of moral critique emerge. In the remainder of the present chapter, I make some general observations relating privacy to the notion of spheres of life.

Thus far we have discussed the crucial role diverse associations and associational ties have in constructing social freedom and social agency. We can begin to think about a sphere of life by identifying a sphere as defined by an associational tie. One important function of privacy is to help maintain the integrity of different spheres of life. Privacy helps maintain both the integrity of intimate spheres as against more public spheres and the integrity of various public spheres in relation to one another. Privacy norms are significant in both connections, because maintaining the integrity of life spheres requires that we have practices that presumptively preclude access to nonrelevant roles of individuals, even when these roles are themselves public.

As already noted, privacy protects intimacy in several ways: It buffers it from certain social control mechanisms that would pressure people to value and regulate personal spheres so as to promote social well-being, as if the exclusive legitimate role of personal parts of life were to contribute to social welfare. Privacy also enables individuals to risk emotional vulnerability through emotional investment, as elaborated in Chapter 1.

Yet the basic unit of regard in social and moral philosophy may be something both bigger and smaller than the individual. It is life spheres or associational ties that exist at this level of analysis, and such spheres are both smaller and larger than the individual. It is smaller in the sense that individuals typically participate in a multitude of spheres of life: nuclear family, extended family, friendships, religious association, work, political party, and so forth. These, in turn, comprise some more restricted spheres. It is larger than the individual because to understand these spheres, we must refer to other people, associated by rules. The model of circles overlapping, where each circle represents a person, is apt here. It displays intersections involving both less and more than one circle. Value is located in these intersections. To recognize these spheres as sources of value we do not have to say that the individual has no value outside the associative ties.

But what we do have to contend with is a mode of thought according to which the dissociated individual is the only source of value, and whatever else has value has it only through realization of the individual will.[4] Even regarding this dissociated individual, it is taken as significant that the will is effective, not because it has anything of particular importance that it must accomplish, but just because it is will gratifying itself. This attitude is more reminiscent of the approach to life exhibited by a three-year-old than by a mature philosopher. How important it is to gratify and indulge the will should be contingent on what exactly the will intends to do with its discretion.

In making this claim we confront directly the esteem with which autonomy is held in so much of modern moral philosophy. Indeed, there is so much about the framework of our lives that we have absolutely or practically no choice about – the time, culture, class, disposition to disease, sex to which we are born – that the choices people do make pale in significance.[5] Second, it is difficult to see how autonomy can even be defended as a value without making it derivative and dependent on some other more clearly recognized objective. Third, there are many things that interfere with important aspects of individual and group life that should be countered. But acknowledging this is very different from thinking that there is something positively of value – choice – that is pursued and is the point of eliminating the impediments.[6]

This penchant for one source of value, and locating this source in autonomy, as exemplified in so much moral theory, does not adequately reflect the value entropy that is at the heart of our world. It places individual will, rather than human relations, at the center of all value, despite the latter being constitutively the key source of human concern for life. Autonomy is treated as the sole source of value even though this focus would surprise the populations of nearly all historical periods and much of the contemporary world. People locate meaning in relationships, in spheres of life, and autonomy can be seen equally as a means to the end rather than as the end that endows those relationships with value. Such a shift in emphasis would model our normative attitudes much more closely than does the standard emphasis. In the next chapter, I illustrate in the context of private life this issue of fit with our attitudes.

In the remainder of this chapter, I show that respecting the integrity of spheres of life is operative in the different public roles that a person might occupy. I do not intend to give the impression that the only sphere of life that is important for people is the intimate sphere. This is not the case. People locate importance in a variety of domains, public as well as private. As I argued in previous chapters, this resource is the basis of whatever social freedom we have. Privacy norms are instrumental in observing the integrity of these spheres as well, even though they are not intimate or personal.

Many of our nonintimate roles, our public roles, are meaningful. To the extent that a person has an important stake in a public role, an argument in terms of social freedom can be made analogous to that made about intimate relationships – that part of what is involved in respecting the person is offering her a measure of immunity from scrutiny and, to the extent feasible, of control vis-à-vis those outside that particular public context. Though the extent of disclosure and investigation will be greater in most public domains than in the domestic realm, some threshold conditions should still be met before a measure of privacy (to be explained) is invaded.

Applying privacy norms in the case of public roles involves

treating public domains of an individual as opaque to one another to the extent feasible. Although sometimes it is not so clear what about a person's particular public role is to be regarded as irrelevant to another public role, when a person is not answerable for behavior in one sphere to anyone outside that sphere, when it is clear that they are unrelated, they should be so treated. To take a controversial example, suppose that a person who has been a successful public school kindergarten teacher for ten years becomes exposed as the national president of a nonviolent but despicable racist organization. Exploring our own reactions to this example will help make my point. If we could be assured that the person really could perform his complex teaching role adequately, in all its subtle dimensions, and his history in teaching should be evidence of this, we would want to say that this other, now public role should have no bearing on our evaluation of his teaching or his qualification as a teacher. This helps to show that we implicitly begin with a presumption that even public spheres should be evaluated as strictly within their own domain as feasible. I confess that, to the extent that a teacher is a role model for students, one could raise questions about this stance. Yet the route of role models suggests one model for people is appropriate in most public domains, and this is just what I wish to counter.

This says more than the tautology that what is not relevant is not relevant. This says that some of what is not narrowly relevant is wrong to introduce into a context. I acknowledge, however, that there are some roles in which such a wide range of factors about other spheres, both public and private, seem relevant, and that in these spheres there would be little that would be wrong to bring up. Public officials and those in certain religious roles, such as that of the pope, we think should do more than handle their jobs efficiently and fairly. They should stand for various things by exhibiting certain qualities of character, even ones not called for in the vast majority of their official tasks. A former top enforcement official at the Securities and Exchange Commission had to leave his job when it was disclosed that he had a long-term pattern of wife abuse. In his role at the SEC, there was no question about how effective he had been. On the other hand, journalists at a conference on privacy[7] indicated that when covering a presidential campaign, they would only reveal embarrassing personal facts about a candidate when these facts related to assessing the political character of a candidate. Thus, much more coverage was warranted of Gary Hart during the 1988 presidential campaign than of other candidates who were having sexual liaisons during the time, because of the way Hart seemed to court danger and display indifference to potential disaster, factors clearly relevant to expectations about running a powerful nation.

People who are politically active and effective may be subject to fewer privacy protections than those not so involved, especially when those active and effective are acting hypocritically. If Senator Jesse Helms of North Carolina was gay, for instance, few would think this information deserved protection, because Helms is so aggressive in influencing policies and patterns of thought that maintain social discrimination against gays.[8] Similarly, if leaders of Operation Rescue, the antiabortion activists, had undergone or arranged abortions earlier in their lives, revelation of this information would be more than an ad hominem attack on their public position. It would reveal real-life difficulties in maintaining what they advocate as the only option.

Why is it important for us to be able to maintain different public roles as separate? One answer to this is that it enhances the opportunities for social freedom for people to restrict their potential influence on others to certain spheres where they interact. There is also a social-dynamics account of this. In his book *The Presentation of Self in Everyday Life*,[9] Erving Goffman argues that audience segregation is necessary to maintain "role credibility." Goffman introduces the notion of "civil inattention" to depict the social pretense that certain pieces of knowledge are not socially operative in certain contexts. Factors in one realm of life are held inoperative when engaging in another; roles define what is relevant and their integrity is breached when irrelevant factors intrude. The moral feature of this situation is as follows: People find it important to their understanding of themselves to occupy diverse roles, both intimate and public. The capacity to occupy these roles depends on one's ability to define a situation socially – to be engaged under a set of rules. These rules make some matters relevant and some inappropriate or even threatening to the role. Thus it is that even in public roles, privacy norms – restricting oneself to limited aspects of another – are important because they are part of what is involved in respecting personality and the role that associational options plays in generating social freedom.

The notion of "minding one's own business" also seems to track the privacy protections I am suggesting occur in public as well as private associations and roles. Unless you and I are connected by associational ties that are relevant, it is not my business how you perform in a role or setting, and trying to make you socially answerable to me would seem at best gratuitous. Leaving you unaccountable to those outside the association for what occurs within limits the social pressure and enhances the social freedom of those so associated.

Let me illustrate this point. Suppose that your and my association is restricted to the employee–employer relationship. I might be curious about how much you read, whether you are a member of the Hemlock Society, whether you and your children are on good terms, whether your diet is high in saturated fats, whether the organization of your union is democratic enough, what, if any, church you regularly attend, and whether you hold office within it, whether you donate money to public television, and so forth. I may think your choice of house colors inappropriate, or that your job is demeaning for a person with your level of education. I may think that your religious affiliations are particularly irrational, that your political and charitable contributions display naïveté, that the people who cut your lawn charge too much for what they do. Because none of these concerns has anything to do with our relationship, they are all clearly none of my business, and your informing me of this is generally appropriate, though potentially risky. Although some of these areas that are off limits to me are clearly within the private domain, some are not private but are related to a public dimension of your life. For instance, if you regularly attend a church, you cannot do so privately. Relative to that community, your attendance is a public act. Another example: In England, among some classes it is regarded as impertinent to ask about a person's employment, although where one is employed certainly falls within a public dimension of life. What seems to be critical in these cases is not the issue of public versus private life but that of associational relevance. Many academics feel that their salaries are none of anyone's business even though those who are state employees recognize that their salaries are paid with public money and are part of the public record.

I wish to dispel the notion that what I am suggesting here is misguided and would, if followed, deprive human relationships, even primarily functional ones, of all human dimensions. Might not it be thought that most of our encounters with others go beyond the role-directed part and display some general regard? Furthermore, it could be objected that I am showing insensitivity to a distinction and thus prejudicing the case. It would be one thing to bring up any of these topics in your yearly evaluation as an employee, but another just to inquire about them as expressing curiosity and personal concern. Furthermore, it could be objected that what is worrisome about any of the examples is the fact that it is an intrusion by one's boss, someone who has power over one.

The thesis I am defending speaks of the boundaries even public roles provide, to people in general, and not just in the case of power differentials. Because, as social beings, we typically care, though to varying degrees, what others think of us, we are vulnerable to some pressure as a result of hoping to avoid judgment by another. Mill and others regard such a vulnerability as oppressive and undermining of social freedom. I regard it as a central ingredient in social freedom for the following reasons.

First, were the employee to overstep his role, this too would be of concern, although the concern is diminished because the employee has less power to injure. Second, we have a notion of "the need to know": Others, we might say, have a right to know, or at least a legitimate interest in knowing, about things relevant to their welfare. It would not follow from another's legitimate interest in knowing something, that we, just in virtue of knowing it, have a duty to tell. Still, we are provided with a reason to offer the information. Inquiries beyond the need to know, unless legitimized by the roles people occupy, overstep boundaries, except when invited. Here life is more subtle than my articulation of its rules can make clear. Part of being socialized in a community involves knowing what the cues are, both verbal and nonverbal, that invite or discourage irrelevant discourse. Whether because a person feels vulnerable or just figures that what is sought is just none of the other's business, we indicate where others should respect domains of our lives.

Much of our life, both public and private, involves us acting in roles that are more or less complete for the purposes of the activity required in the role. These role boundaries have a point and facilitate interaction by being kept within terms of the role expectations. These boundaries also enhance prospects for social freedom. As I argue in the next chapter, these boundaries are as important to observe in private relationships as they are in public relationships.

Chapter 10

Spheres of life:
a literary exploration

In Chapters 6 and 7, I discussed the social dynamics of the boundaries between various associative and functional ties. We saw there that the degree of transparency of these boundaries both influenced and was influenced by the degree of social control present or deemed desirable. The more it is thought that people within one domain of life ought to be free from social control by those not associated within the domain, the more opaque the boundaries. The more people regard some activity within a domain as important to control at all costs, or the more people realize that pressures from within a domain are inadequate to achieve important social objectives, the more transparent the boundaries. Activity within a domain I labeled a 'sphere of life.' I developed the relationship between social freedom and privacy, interpreting privacy norms as limiting access, both observational and regulative, to a person. This limited access was characterized as a many-place relationship: It is relative to given people, in a given situation, within a given domain, and to a given capacity.

In the preceding chapter, I argued that analysis of social life in terms of this depiction of privacy affords us a better tool for understanding our privacy practices than does the standard public–private distinction. Privacy limits access to people not only in their private lives but in nearly all the domains of their lives. If we think of a spectrum of domains, it is not only those characterized as part of private life that are governed by privacy norms. Many of these domains are private vis-à-vis other domains even if none of the domains is located in what we would normally call a person's private sphere. For instance, how I perform as a volunteer coach for the neighborhood swim team is not appropriate for decision making at my place of work.

Generally speaking, activity in one sphere is normatively private vis-à-vis another. Some matters, however, are so serious that even though they occur within one sphere, it is appropriate to take notice from the perspective of other spheres. This measure may be necessary to maintain the appropriate level of control of behavior in that sphere.

Even if we have multiple relationships with a person, the context of the sphere of interaction makes some things out of bounds that would be appropriate in the other sphere, were that the one that was operative. In this respect, private life is no different from public life. Both public and private life are themselves partitioned into multiple spheres, each sphere constituted by rules and roles or relationships. Most of these spheres, if not all of them, have an integrity to them, a theme I will explore in this chapter.

The partition of life into spheres is not the only parameter of analysis of privacy, even though this partition is sufficient to generate privacy norms. For as we saw in Chapter 1, private life is differentiated from public life along ways not operative in demarcating one public sphere from another. Some of the features that characterize private dimensions are distinct from public dimensions of life. Those more representative of private spheres than public spheres include the extent of emotional vulnerability, the extent of inner rather than external and functional focus, the dominance of relationships over roles in ideals of organization, the richer dimensions of the self that are involved. So, although there will be different social dynamics in small stable groups than there are in large, unstable ones, size and stability are not the only factors that differentiate private from public spheres of life.

Having explored in previous chapters how privacy helps

structure public life, I consider in this chapter how privacy structures private life. Specifically, I examine how morality in private spheres functions differently than does morality in public spheres. What emerges from this discussion is the extent to which the contours of morality typically portrayed in moral theory belong to that branch of morality that regulates public spheres. Because most of our active moral dealings arise in the private domain, the identification of morality with public-sphere morality reflects a misguided emphasis as well as a biased supply of paradigms for moral thinking generally. For source material for the examination of private life we will turn to some of Henry James's fiction.

Several points that challenge standard moral conceptions emerge from our focus on private spheres of life: (1) Although moral philosophy is largely focused on establishing the centrality of autonomy to human moral being, it is not our independence from others but our connections to them that account for the skills we value. Furthermore, these connections make our life a human life. (2) Morality, in the sense that philosophers discuss it, applies primarily to contexts involving others in relationships that presuppose the interchangeability of persons; it focuses on maintaining institutions or goals, not particular, individuated relationships. Morality in a public context is primarily rule-oriented, with the rules deriving from institutional role responsibilities. (3) Private morality, in contrast, maintains stable relationships between particular people and, to this end, discretion, flexibility, and creativity are appropriate in assessing what is permissible or right.[1] Morality in this private sphere is oriented toward character and motivation as much as to performance. (4) Our scruples about the dignity of individuals are models for understanding the integrity of spheres of life.

Overall, people in private spheres are enmeshed in ways possibly not characteristic of public spheres. Our understanding of morality and especially our understanding of privacy should reflect this associational or relational core to our lives. In discussing this I hope to redeem the claim I made at several points in earlier chapters about the relationship between privacy and interpersonal intimacy. Many analyses of privacy stress the relationship between privacy and separation. Separation is always part of privacy, but as I explained, it is also part of public spheres as well. The separation in private life is functional, characteristically serving the end of facilitating connection, intimacy.

Although it is important to say more about what is meant by a 'sphere of life,' at present I make only two observations. One is that the concept is not value neutral or purely descriptive. We see something as a sphere when we think that it organizes our life or relationships in an intrinsically valuable way. Second, if we think of a sphere of life as something that differentiates friendships, profession, social life, and religious associations, we will have too coarse a picture. Within these domains there are subdomains that play the role of spheres. Different types of friendship or even individual intimate relationships might each count as a sphere. Each sphere is bounded by privacy norms. We are not free to treat every friendship as transparent to any other.

The preceding chapter suggested the importance of keeping different spheres of life distinct and recognizing the integrity of only part of a person. The plausibility of this claim depends on the position that people are multidimensional and dependent on multiple associations for their freedom and well-being. Each of these dimensions and associations calls for a measure of respect, even from the agent herself, who identifies with these multiple loyalties.

Consider a person with diverse dimensions and loyalties, each rich with inherent value. Managing such a life involves a moral economy comparable with political morality; both require some method of balancing the interests of different spheres without treating any as if unimportant.

If we think of spheres of life as having an integrity of their own, of having internal or intrinsic principles, and of being largely unordered – no fixed priority rules – we get a more accurate picture of how individuals actually experience life. Life has diverse spheres, each of which has an integrity. Respecting one sphere leaves other spheres intact.

Henry James offers us a picture of life that we can use to support and elaborate the claims I have been making about the moral structure of private life. Our consideration includes *The Golden Bowl*, "The Aspern Papers," and *The Portrait of a Lady*. Because we shall be dealing with moral issues in the context of what purports to be life, the points I wish to make will not emerge in systematic order.

The Golden Bowl deals exclusively with private – indeed with domestic – dimensions of lives. All the main characters are related by blood or marriage. The world depicted is by no means narrow or unvariegated because of this. It is rich with complex relationships and psychological struggle. Nor does the confined topic make privacy or respect for independent spheres less significant. Indeed, it makes privacy all the more prominent, because there are so many intense fundamental and interconnected relationships that must be maintained that any acknowledged break in the outer seam of one would wreak havoc on the whole. Each individual relationship must be maintained with a certain character, and effecting this end requires considerable creative resources, including, most notably, privacy.

The novel covers four years in the lives of four people: Maggie Verver, an American expatriate living in London, daughter of a wealthy widower; Adam Verver, Maggie's father, who is an art collector in the process of setting up a gallery in the United States; Amerigo, an Italian prince, who must make a good marriage in order to sustain his own honor and his family's traditions; and Charlotte Stant, an American, a friend of Maggie.

The novel begins with Maggie's marriage to the prince imminent. Unbeknownst to Maggie, Charlotte and Amerigo had shared an intense, loving relationship that could not result in a marriage because of Charlotte's and the prince's lack of means. Before the marriage takes place, Charlotte arrives in London and arranges to meet the prince for a private stroll during which she reveals that she came from America just hoping to spend a few hours alone with him. The prince is cool to these overtures but refrains from telling

Maggie of the meeting, presumably because a full account would disclose his intimate history with Charlotte.

Once the marriage between Maggie and the prince occurs, and the couple return from an extended foreign visit, the pattern of their life settles in a way that has Maggie as solicitous of, and devoted to, her father as she ever was. Although she loves, even reveres, the prince, her main emotional preoccupation is assuring herself that her father will not suffer a loss of intimacy as a result of her marriage. Maggie encourages her father to court and marry Charlotte as a way of ensuring his personal welfare. Adam Verver, in a mixture of attraction for Charlotte and desire to pacify his daughter, does marry Charlotte. Ironically, because Charlotte is able and willing to spend time with the prince, Maggie becomes even less restrained in devoting attention to her father. Charlotte and the prince are aware of their limited places in the lives of their respective spouses. Through some prompting from Charlotte, they reengage their intimate and secret relationship.

Now that the relationships of these four characters are sufficiently precarious, a new, destabilizing force emerges: Maggie's efforts at understanding her place. Initially, she rejoices that she has found a love from whom she holds nothing back while at the same time promoting her father's comfort.

> She had been able to marry without breaking, as she liked to put it, with her past. She had surrendered herself to her husband without the shadow of a reserve or a condition, and yet she had not, all the while, given up her father by the least little inch. She had compassed the high felicity of seeing the two men beautifully take to each other, and nothing in her marriage had marked it as more happy than this fact of its having practically given the elder, the lonelier, a new friend. What had moreover all the while enriched the whole aspect of success was that the latter's marriage had been no more measurably paid for than her own. His having taken the same great step in the same free way had not in the least involved

relegation of his daughter. That it was remarkable that they should have been able at once so to separate and so to keep together had never for a moment, from however far back, been equivocal to her. (Book II, Part IV, Chapter 25)

Several realizations suggest to Maggie that her preferred picture fails to correspond to reality. First, she thinks that the conformity of her ideal with reality in her domestic world is oddly perfect – perfect in a way that one should know life too rarely allows. Second, Maggie entertains the suspicion that really she may have abandoned her husband through her degree of intimacy with her father, leaving only what must seem to him a secondary position in her life. Third, Maggie notes that Charlotte and the prince characteristically respond to their neglect with an indulgence suggesting that they are playing well-orchestrated parts. If she and her father have abandoned their respective spouses, why don't they express concern? Why are they content with so little? Why do they respond always so as to protect Maggie's and Adam's sense of perfection?

After months of silent brooding, confirmation of her suspicions presents itself at her door. An antique dealer from whom Maggie has bought a golden bowl comes to her house to rectify the transaction. There he recognizes the photographs of Charlotte and Amerigo as those of a couple who had previously spent time in his shop, considering the very golden bowl that Maggie bought. The dealer can place the event at a time that Maggie knows to be just days before her married to Amerigo. Amerigo never mentioned this meeting, let alone the familiarity with Charlotte presupposed by it. Had Maggie known of this, she probably would still have married Amerigo, but she never would have dreamed of encouraging a marriage between Charlotte and her father, especially because of the close bonds she expected to maintain between her father's life and her own.

Once Maggie assures herself that she *knows* that she has been deceived by Amerigo and Charlotte, both about the past and the present, she has various relationships to deal with, each on its own separate terms: her relationship with Amerigo, which must change as a result of her discovery; her relationship with her father, which must continue to be protective of him; her relationship with Charlotte, which must change but not in its "public," acknowledged aspect; her father's relationship with Charlotte, which she wants to protect and improve; her father's relationship to the prince, which is to be protected; and finally Charlotte's relationship with the prince, which she wants to cool. Maggie appreciates the enormous finesse it will take to protect both her father and her own marriage.

Maggie realizes that by merely telling the prince what she now knows, his relationships to her and Charlotte will undergo dramatic movement. The prince cares a great deal for appearances and respects the mastery over an environment knowledge affords. Maggie's discovery will require that the prince change his estimation of her, bringing them to a new level of intimacy, respect, and trust. This opens an avenue for Maggie's influence in restructuring the prince's and Charlotte's relationship. The prince is now to keep Charlotte in the dark about Maggie's realization, signifying contempt for Charlotte and a repudiation of the integrity of their intimacy. Maggie accomplishes this maneuver not by explicit requests for concessions and confessions. Instead, her strategy relies on her trust that the prince, in return for her respect for his need to maintain appearances and reserve, will be naturally attuned both to discern and to effect what would best accomplish her objectives.

Maggie's hand has to be played subtly, because any open rupture will have devastating consequences for her father. This entails reticence on her part when dealing with her father and a policy of avoidance and denial when dealing with Charlotte. In one of the very powerful scenes in the book, one displaying Maggie's control over herself and others, Charlotte confronts Maggie and asks whether she has offended her in any way. Maggie assures Charlotte that she doesn't feel she has suffered the slightest wrong and reinforces this by saying that her assurance can be taken as a matter of honor. Charlotte asks for a kiss to seal this assurance and herself offers one. Earlier, on his honor, the prince had assured Charlotte that nothing had changed between them and that Maggie still knew nothing of their affair. These factors – Charlotte's pretense, insincerity, and probable self-deception in thinking of herself as faultless, and the contempt Maggie and the prince display toward her – reveal the extent of Charlotte's moral alienation and social isolation. One can appreciate Charlotte's suffering and her overall situation of not being a priority on anyone's intimate list, but she is a person who never redeems herself as a moral agent and seems incapable of coming to terms with herself. Not only is she capable of asking Maggie if she has offended her after she, while married to Maggie's father, has begun an affair with Maggie's husband, but she later accuses Maggie of trying to subvert her relationship with Adam. Charlotte has a legitimate concern, but her manner of responding to it threatens nearly every dimension of the private environment of the four characters. From Maggie's perspective, Charlotte must be indulged in her self-deception because allowing her to see herself as a mere victim is the best means of protecting Charlotte's relationship with Adam. In seeing herself as undermined in her relationship to Adam by Maggie, she will realize that her best chances lie in going elsewhere with Adam to find a life less intense in its extended family intimacies.

What does this drama illustrate about privacy and spheres of life? First, we see a plenitude of relationships, most of which seem worth protecting because of the meaning the intimacy has provided for the characters. This is part of what is meant by respecting the integrity of each sphere. Even the intimacy that is morally troublesome, the secret relationship between Charlotte and the prince, strikes this reader, and I suppose most, as having its own integrity. One must feel troubled by the prince's lack of candor toward Charlotte; there is something repugnant and dishonorable about his disavowing his relationship to her without explanation and with aggravated deception. Their relationship, illicit though it was, means that Charlotte is owed more. It is precisely this moral cost that the prince exploits to show Maggie how much he is willing to do for her. We could not do justice to this story unless we were prepared to recognize the multiple relationships that exist within the private lives of these characters. However undifferentiated private life looks from the Olympian vantage of the political or public perspective, once within the private domain, one sees that there are enormous contours, discontinuities, and borders, each defining distinct spheres with their own intrinsic characters and requirements.

Second, in the literary setting, one sees clearly the contrast between normally recognized moral requirements and the demands of relationships in which everyone is immersed to some extent. The latter call for personal judgment and creative resolution based on a sensitivity to the complexities of the situation that only rarely could be explained or adequately justified to an uninformed, indifferent, and hurried public. Private life is more dynamic and involves subtler and more nuanced principles than does public life. Maggie and the others cannot limit their responses to those specifically called for by their roles. In a sense her role could be played by ignoring what is happening to her husband and forgoing expectations of personal fulfillment in life with the prince. It is because she is seeking something personal involving others that her response or strategy must fit exactly the people concerned.

Third, Maggie is not insulated from responsibility for the total outcome, even though this outcome involves other responsible agents and depends on factors she cannot control. Nor is she restricted in what she is to consider in seeking a resolution. These factors contrast sharply with public role behavior. For instance, at times, the lawyer is obliged to defend the guilty, the physician is obliged to save the vicious, the employer is obliged to fire the incompetent, and the policeman to evict the needy – all this without holding themselves accountable for the larger ramifications of their acts. Public judgment and public roles must limit themselves to manifest and incomplete features of a situation. Complex social organization depends upon such a demarcation of responsibility. Competing considerations may be appreciated, but typically a higher threshold must be met in public roles than in private roles before the role responsibilities are outweighed by these considerations. These competing considerations, which seem external to the public role, are more internal to the private role where divisions and contrasts are less sharp. Managing private affairs requires much more feeling for detail and sensitivity to ambiguities.

Private spheres are concerned with subtler aspects of life than can be aimed at through public roles. Maggie wants the prince to be *her husband*, not just someone who lives with her and abstains from intimacies with others. In intimate spheres, we interact with specific others in the context of relationships, not with generic or fungible others as often typifies our public encounters and as defined by roles.[2] Private morality aims at maintaining, restoring, or restructuring a balance in continuing relationships between the same parties that endure from episode to episode. It is their relationship, and not the grand designs of an institution or practice, that is to be maintained. Although the meaning of private relations is greatly informed by their institutional context, it is not the purposes of the larger context that constitute the ends of the relationship, but rather it is the relationship itself. Maggie's behavior is not to be understood by alluding to her interest in families in general but by her dependence on her relationships with Amerigo and her father.

In contrast, within the public context, the characters in particular roles or offices are normally interchangeable. Maintaining this possibility significantly limits the discretion and creativity any given role occupant can exercise. The acts must be justifiable to others in terms limited by institutional objectives and, to some extent, general social norms.

I have just suggested that privacy norms may operate most prominently in the domains in which characters are not replaceable and where it is a priority to maintain relationships among them for the relationships' own sake. Conventional morality characteristically gets engaged in maintaining *insti-*

tutions or *structures*, not relationships – or at least not those relationships that require considerable finesse with a relatively constant cast of characters. I return to this theme in the discussion of *The Portrait of a Lady*, which shows how destructive it can be to treat someone in a personal relationship as if what were really most significant was the structure itself.

Another way to consider this dichotomy between the structures of private and public morality is to see private spheres as arenas in which individuals make the development of something meaningful for themselves a priority. To achieve this, a finely tuned accommodation must take place so that individuals' lives mesh on an especially personal, individual level – a level in which they have invested a lot of themselves and one in which they become especially vulnerable. In this domain, they are to care about others in their particularity and they are in turn to be cared for in their own individuality. Recall here Max Scheler's distinction, introduced in Chapter 1, between being treated as an abstract other where only one facet is considered, compared with being treated as a whole person. Because private life is the sphere in which individuals relate as individuals, and because maintaining relationships between individuals as individuals is more demanding than maintaining relationships between individuals as generic role players or officeholders, we grant greater discretion in private than in public domains. We feel less competent to judge right and wrong in private domains, and we set higher thresholds before scrutiny and intervention are deemed legitimate. Even when the threshold for scrutiny and intervention is transgressed, because a personal relationship is at issue, we still recognize the domain as private, despite letting outsiders intervene. The privacy norms are still engaged, and we have a proclivity to aim at restoring the personal relationship on a more fitting basis through our intervention, if that is possible.

Seeing things this way helps explain something about the relationship of privacy to morality generally. I mentioned in Chapter 1 that all domains of life are rule-governed, and that includes private domains. On the account offered here, we acknowledge that private life is rule-governed in a sense, but that the rules are not exhausted by listing popular morality's clichés. The objective of maintaining meaningful relationships with specific, given individuals, and the need to locate meaning in life through these relationships remains. These factors transform the kind of morality involved in private life.[3] In private life generally, and in intimate life particularly, something more than rule-conforming behavior is required. Attitudes, motivations, sensibilities, and vulnerabilities are at least as much at issue as behavior. We want to connect with others in certain relationships, in addition to being participants in certain patterns of interaction; we want these connections to ground these patterns. To a much larger extent, in institutional contexts, rule conformity suffices.

Someone might object to the contrast suggested between making moral judgments in the private realm and making moral judgments in the public realm. Many public decisions are certainly complex and delicate: controversial court decisions, arms negotiations, the formulation of welfare and defense policies. What could be more complex than these? One factor these sensitive public decisions share with private decision making is the considerable discretion and latitude countenanced in their resolution. In both cases, resolutions involve more than following rules, and so they assume a creative dimension. We do not think that public officials, in their capacities as such, should have loyalty to anything but the public good. In the case of private relationships, we think that while the public good is in some vague way limiting, it is the personal and inner focus that *should* preoccupy the participants. In a public role, ideally one represents an institution or others generally, *whatever* the personal effects. In a private relationship, one represents dimensions of oneself. Even the subtlest social issue differs from issues that arise in the private domain in that we expect individuals in their private spheres to find some kind of accommodation between their own natural prompting and their connections to others. In other words, an ideal of character development is implicit in private spheres. In the public sector, it is entirely other-directed virtues that are required. Finally, in the public sphere, because individuals who play certain roles are generally replaceable, universal implications can be drawn from any given right decision. To the extent that the irreplaceability of people plays a bigger role in an encounter or relationship, the dominance of general principles that neatly decide all cases dissipates. Thus in private life there is more scope than in public life for the assessment that something right for one person is wrong for another, similarly situated.

To explore a further dimension of private morality that emerges from the novel, with its emphasis on relationships, we will consider some details of encounters between Maggie and a friend, Fanny. Once Maggie begins to wonder and torment herself about the prince and Charlotte, she confides in Fanny about her suspicions. Fanny, it turns out, knows about Charlotte and Amerigo's earlier relationship and about the adulterous affair between them. Nevertheless, Fanny lies to Maggie, reassuring her repeatedly that her despair and fears are groundless. Fanny's motivation in lying stems from her confidence in Maggie: She believes that the situation can be passably resolved only if the resolution evolves from Maggie's unaided understanding and creative goodness. Curiously, once Maggie comes to recognize the truth and then finds out that Fanny knew all along, she does not berate Fanny. Rather, she takes Fanny's deceit as evidence of Fanny's deep affection and trust.

From the perspective of contemporary moral theory, with its emphasis on autonomy and the informed decision making that autonomy requires, Fanny's deceit would be problematic, a prima facie assault on Maggie's dignity.[4] In the novel, Fanny's confidence in Maggie's personal resources illustrates her respect for Maggie and the factors that give Maggie's life meaning. In other words, it is wrong to see Maggie as an isolated individual toward whom respect can be shown independent of other things. To respect as well as care for Maggie *is* to see her as part of a constellation of relationships, and to measure what to do in terms of that larger complex. Maggie understands this, sees herself in the same way, and hence never questions the decency and respect *for her* evidenced by Fanny's duplicity. Fanny's relationship with Maggie is one of friendship, not of agency. The sort of trust involved in friendship or intimacy has more flexibility and discretion that would only be denied if we take promotion of autonomy to be the end that dominates all others in all contexts.

Another aspect of dependencies that arise in private life, largely absent from public life, is also exemplified in the novel. In private life, antagonists and protagonists largely share the same fates. Public and political conflicts rarely exemplify such abiding dependencies. Furthermore, expectations are so much more intense in private than in public spheres, because of the degree to which the participants' identities mesh. Judgments in private spheres are made in situations where continuing relationships must be taken as the dominant end. These same people must be lived with after the inevitable crises, and that means that strategies of dealing with conflict must be different than in the public realm. Maggie's spheres of concern require maintaining multilateral relationships. This factor further explains why private and public morality must be organized in different ways. The motivations, expectations, and consequences of conflicts are so different.

In private life, the most important factors, intimacy and congruence, must result from trust and self-knowledge. Practices that ensure external enforcement impede the chances for these qualities to emerge. The objective of a private sphere is a life shaped by, and shared with, another – not some further envisioned end to which the life together is made subservient or secondary. This is a major reason why intimate spheres and public spheres are structured by different principles and strategies.

For many contexts, individuals will reliably comply with preestablished rules and conventions to facilitate and normalize interactions, and thereby improve efficiency. In these contexts, neither relationships nor self-expression, but some product or goal, such as aprons, fixed faucets, or greater productivity, is the object. Efficiency is maximized in these settings by minimizing opportunities for negotiating what the governing rules are; requiring or even tolerating such negotiation in advance would complicate interactions unless long-term exchange is at issue. Certain things can be done that are of mutual benefit if the parties, without knowing one another, can count on certain procedures being followed.

Admittedly there are management styles employed in some public and business spheres that do stress flexibility and discretion. But even when these styles are recommended, there is an external objective completely independent of the relationship that is used to assess the value of the relationship style. Private spheres are less subject to review by standards that are so clearly external to the relationship.

But not all our encounters are of this sort. Sometimes we deal with the same people over time, and there are advantages to both the parties and their relationships in negotiating the rules. Without time, knowledge, and trust, the negotiations would be inefficient; but with these factors, people can smooth out certain inherent disadvantages that are features of fixed rules. So not only are the rules for intimate relationships likely to be different than the rules for social and business relationships generally, but *the relationship to the rules themselves* is likely to be different. In intimate relationships, rules are negotiable for mutual advantage. There is an opportunity to have a relationship and not just a role.

Successful accommodation over time increases trust and intuitive initiative. Recall the deceit that Fanny employed in giving Maggie time to deal with her problem, and the strategy that Maggie engaged to reestablish her husband's loyalty. Each of these had to be creative but silent moves in the context of the relationship; explicit negotiation would have been self-defeating. Because the parties see themselves as committed to the relationship, they will tolerate and appreciate fluidity in the rules, and see this fluidity as constructive.

Developing a relationship requires being successful at customizing the rules to the participants. We think of people who are uncomfortable or poor at these skills as ill-suited to personal relationships, just as we see people who use personal relationships to get something for themselves in a way exclusive of sharing life with another. The new rules and their very possibility define part of what the personal relationship is. It presupposes trust, goodwill, and continued interaction. Private life, like public life, is rule-governed. But the rules are of a different sort and are fashioned with different goals in mind.

The confining and inner focus of intimate relationships also accounts for the phenomenological feature that spheres of life are largely unordered. To impose an ordering, and to keep it in one's awareness, is to qualify intimate relationships in a way that seems inimical to their integrity. Of course, some of our spheres we see as secondary, even from inside the sphere. Nevertheless, many of our spheres are seen from within as unconditioned or unconditional. Morality, religion, friendship, family, nationality – these are often seen as unbounded in their range, even though on reflection we would acknowledge their potential conflict with one another, let alone with other matters of value.[5] Seeing a sphere as unbounded is part of what is involved in thinking of its having integrity. It fully represents one aspect of the person that is not beholden to external legitimizing objectives.

To illustrate this point, consider Maggie's relationships to her father and husband. Although through much of the book the latter relationship suffers because of the former, it would not be right to say that Maggie thinks of her relationship with her father as more important than her relationship with Amerigo. When Maggie realizes the importance of the two couples separating geographically, she does not see this as demoting her father or that relationship in her estimation. Indeed, in large part it is for his sake, as well as for that of the others, that the separation becomes necessary.

"Pure sentimentalism!" someone might charge. "The ordering must be there, even if people find it inconvenient or upsetting to make it explicit. How else would conflicts among different spheres ever be resolved?"

Other factors besides priority rankings may explain our resolutions when conflicts arise between private spheres. One might make a decision on the basis of what one's responsibilities are, or even on what the utilities are, without thinking that either solution reflects a *personal ranking* of these relationships.

Many philosophers and decision theorists treat such a solution as just another personal constraint on decisions. One does not *personally* abandon one sphere for the benefit of promoting values in another. The agent's own ranking is not settled by these external rules, even though they reflect the agent's own acknowledgment of these rules' authority for ordering life. The encouragement to treat recognition of authority as reflecting an agent's personal ranking is symptomatic of a behavioristic perspective on judgment. This perspective fails to reflect a critical component of judgment. We saw earlier how failure to recognize legitimacy of authorities besides the isolated individual's personal judgment is endemic to a whole style of philosophical reflection.

The recognition of an external authority affecting one's choices, without affecting one's preferences, may be compared with language use. What I mean by uttering "The phone is ringing," is in large part determined by what this sentence means in the language. It cannot be analyzed by exclusive reference to my own mental states, even though what is at issue is my meaning. In both the choice setting and the meaning setting, analyses that refuse to countenance external authorities just miss that component of human affairs.

By not ordering or exploiting one's spheres, one regards them as having integrity. We can gain some insight into this by looking at "The Aspern Papers." In this tale, a literary critic, never named, has devoted his life to the study of a deceased poet, Jeffrey Aspern. The private papers of this revered poet are assumed by the critic to be in the possession of the poet's very aged, former mistress, Juliana Bordereau. Miss Juliana lives a secluded life in an old villa in Venice, which she shares with her middle-aged, unworldly, unwed niece, Miss Tita. Miss Juliana has been approached in the past for these papers, but all approaches have been rebuffed. The critic is confident that no further headway can be made in the understanding of this poet without these papers, and he thus regards finding these papers a sacred mission, worth every sacrifice.

The critic hits on a strategy: He will venture to Venice and seek lodging in the villa, and so position himself to acquire what he needs. He approaches the villa, makes his offer to Miss Tita to rent a room and manage the garden, has a brief interview with the awesome Miss Juliana, and finds his offer accepted. Although he eventually enlists the confidence, and to a certain extent the help, of Miss Tita in seeking to accomplish his purpose, he realizes that Miss Juliana is an estimable opponent, one unlikely to misjudge where her real interests lie. After months of probing he has little to show for it, except a heightened confidence that the papers he seeks are indeed somewhere in the inner chambers of Miss Juliana's apartment. But he also becomes increasingly fearful that Miss Juliana is quite aware of his scheme and will secretly destroy the papers, while keeping him on as a paying – a dearly paying – boarder. What she might really want from him, he discovers only later.

In his anguish over his dimming prospects, one evening when Miss Juliana seems not to be in her chambers, the critic starts to poke about, checking to see which drawers are locked – just, he says to himself, to get a better sense of his options but not really to pry. Miss Juliana, coming from nowhere, confronts him probing her inner sanctum.

> Miss Bordereau stood there in her nightdress, in the doorway of her room, watching me; her hands were raised, she had lifted the everlasting curtain that covered half her face, and for the first, the last, the only time I beheld her extraordinary eyes. They glared at me, they made me horribly ashamed. I

183

never shall forget her strange little bent tottering figure, with
its lifted head, her attitude, her expression; neither shall I
forget the tone in which as I turned, looking at her, she hissed
out passionately, furiously,
"Ah, you publishing scoundrel."

Miss Juliana collapses, and the critic flees the villa, burdened
with the suspicion that he caused her death.

Days later, he drifts back and finds out from Miss Tita that
Miss Juliana has indeed died. He then wants to know
whether Aspern's papers are still safe. Miss Tita assures him
that they are, but begins to hint that there is a price to be
paid for them, out of respect for Miss Juliana's wishes. Miss
Juliana, full of concern that her niece be taken care of, could
be presumed willing that the critic acquire the papers, provided that he marry Miss Tita: "It went without saying that
I could not pay the price. I could not accept. I could not, for
a bundle of tattered papers, marry a ridiculous, pathetic,
provincial old woman."

Again, the critic flees with a sense of horror, this time
occasioned by the outrageous offer. But with time, he re-
considers. He reminds himself how much it would mean to
him to gain possession of these papers.

> They were more precious than ever, and a kind of ferocity had
> come into my desire to possess them. The condition Miss Tita
> had attached to the possession of them no longer appeared an
> obstacle worth thinking of, and for an hour, that morning, my
> repentant imagination brushed it aside.

The critic then reapproaches Miss Tita to pursue the possibilities of accepting the marriage offer and gaining access
to the papers. He finds out that she has burned them, "one
by one." The critic and Miss Tita part company for good.

In this narrative, the critic has one overriding goal in life
that structures all his other concerns. Throughout the story
he engages in a series of questionable moves to achieve his
end. Not only was he engaged in a form of undercover work
that involved the most intimate kind of prying into the life

of another, living in her home over a period of months under completely false pretenses for an end she would find unwelcome in the extreme, but he even rummages through her private drawers; his very efforts in testing to see if the drawers are locked causes her death. None of this chastens our critic. When the prospect of acquiring the papers is offered, provided he will marry Miss Tita, his own initial abhorrence saves him from even further wrongs – both to himself and to Miss Tita. He could not become her husband without doing violence to intimate dimensions of both Miss Tita and himself. He wants the papers desperately, and just as desperately she wants to be cared for; a marriage would accomplish both. But a marriage would also have a dynamic of its own that would make itself felt, probably demolishing both parties in the process.

It is a platitude that life is full of little sacrifices. So what would be wrong with the proposed marriage? After all, as far as the reader can tell, he and Miss Tita alike have no romantic alternatives.

Given all the other unprincipled things the critic does to get the papers, his rejection of this offer has particular power, highlighting the depth and emotional significance *for him* of the social definition of marriage. It is significant that the critic recognized limited control over what a marriage is to be. We saw in Chapter 7 that perhaps for most of human history and prehistory, marriages were not vested with expectations of intimacy. The fact of the variability of the institution over time and culture in no way affords individuals flexibility in structuring relations as they choose. Socialization works against that possibility, just as it would work against people in the thirteenth century trying to have a late twentieth-century marriage.

On reflection, the critic comes to think that he can afford to add another violation to his list, but his instinctive sense of revulsion shows that what he would be transgressing is not just something that *other* people value. To see a marriage as something with merely instrumental value aimed at an objective totally independent of intimacy or caring would be unthinkable, reckless, destructive, horrible. Notably, when the critic changes his mind, it is not because he comes to see the marriage differently; rather he comes to feel more comfortable with the thought of sinking, once again, for the sake of the papers.

The prospect of marriage is incinerated by the same flame that consumes the papers. What otherwise might have occurred if the form of intimacy had been exploited? *The Portrait of a Lady* examines such a marriage.

The basics of the story are as follows: While still in her late teens, Isabel Archer, an American whose parents had died, is visited by her aunt and invited to accompany her on her travels to England and the continent. Isabel accepts and stays on at her aunt's and uncle's estate in England.

Rather than settling down with a husband and raising a family, Isabel is determined to experience the world for herself. Before she turns twenty, she has rebuffed two passionate suitors for her hand in marriage – one a successful American businessman and another an English lord. Before her uncle dies, his son persuades him to bestow much of his fortune on Isabel.

Thus Isabel inherits a vast fortune. An acquaintance of Isabel's, Madame Merle, a woman Isabel comes to trust and admire as much as anyone, introduces Isabel to a widower whom she suspects will take an interest in Isabel. This widower, Gilbert Osmond, is an expatriate American, living in Italy on a meager income. Osmond has exquisite tastes in art and culture generally, but no means to pursue this passion. Osmond has a child, Pansy, who is actually the issue of a long-past affair between Osmond and Madame Merle. Madame Merle has an interest in Osmond marrying someone, because then her child will find a source of active love. Gilbert is too rigid and insensitive to offer his daughter anything but repression and imprisonment in a convent school that teaches resignation, acquiescence, and propriety. After meeting Isabel, Osmond does come to have an interest in Isabel, because the resources she can afford him would enable him to live in a style fitting a person with his cultural sensibilities. For reasons to be explored later, Isabel also finds herself attracted to Osmond.

After a year and a half of travel, Isabel returns to Italy and marries Osmond. Before long, Isabel finds that Osmond is not the sort of person who can have a relationship with another person. He has contempt for her opinions, her energy, her excitement in life, her friends – everything about her. Much of the novel deals with Isabel's disintegration in the context of this disastrous match. The only virtue Isabel can see in her "relationship" to Osmond is the support she can offer Pansy and the dignity she gains for herself by acquiescing in the consequences of her own mistaken judgment.

Osmond acts in personal contexts oblivious to the sharing and understanding that structure intimacy. The problem is not that he uses his marriage to Isabel to achieve his private objectives – perhaps all marriages aim at something like this – but the objectives take no account of her as a person: her outlook, her values, her vulnerabilities, her aspirations, her satisfactions. All that matters to him is that she can adorn his life and help him achieve his preexisting objectives. No part of his objectives is altered by his marriage to Isabel. The fact that his wife is Isabel Archer makes no difference to him.

He judges by conventions and forms. He relates only to what he can isolate and control for the sake of his vision. His level of appreciation for the conventional and traditional and his disregard for the personal conjointly put him in the category of sociopathic agents – undaunted by the prospect of breaking the souls of those dependent upon him for emotional and personal support.

Everything Osmond does in connection with his wife and daughter he does consulting only his own sense of propriety, relying for his rationale completely on the form of what it is to have the authority of a father or husband. Taking a personal regard for the perspective of either his wife or daughter never occurs to him.

The most chilling aspect of Gilbert's defiling influence is the practical success he has in getting Isabel to betray her own sense of propriety and decency to promote his ends. This comes out poignantly in three scenes. In the first, we find Isabel counseling Pansy, her beloved and loving step-daughter, to respect her father's wishes to give up the man she loves so that her father can find a better match for her – meaning by "better" one that better fits *his* vision of his place in the social universe. Anytime Pansy needs a push to free her from her father's will, Isabel degrades herself by representing Osmond's interests. Isabel subjects her relationship to Pansy to her role vis-à-vis Gilbert. Because Pansy loves Isabel so much, Isabel's admonitions are all the more effective – all the more destructive (chapter 45).

The second scene portrays an incident that occurs at the end of the novel reminiscent of the one just described. When Isabel has the opportunity to liberate Pansy, now a twenty-year-old, from a convent to which her father has sent her in order to facilitate his absolute domination over her emotional and moral life, Isabel counsels obedience (chapter 52). The third scene reveals a picture of Isabel's life with Osmond: She tells her husband, "We don't live decently together!" (chapter 51). Because he judges by forms alone, Osmond probably does not understand this as a reproach. For Isabel, it expresses the alienation between the core of life and its formal structures, an alienation that condemns her to an abject emotional state.

The power of Osmond's hostility to intimate content is evidenced in his subjugation of Isabel, strong and independent as she is revealed before her marriage to Gilbert. Although she betrays everything she regards as decent in herself for her sense of marital propriety, she suffers the tragedy of realizing what she involuntarily contributes to. Here we can mention, as an illustration of the earlier point about ordering loyalties, that Isabel does not regard her other concerns as less worthy than her conception of marital loyalty, but only not available options for her to address in light of her role responsibilities. Her experience of self-betrayal could not be made intelligible otherwise.

Earlier in this chapter I drew a distinction between relationships that aim at intimacy and those that aim to maintain or support a structure or institution. One of the factors that fixes Isabel to the relationship with Osmond despite the enormous costs is her loyalty to the institution of marriage itself. This engages her sense of honor, and she carefully protects the public image she thinks a marriage should project.

Henry James expresses skepticism that such sacrifices as Isabel makes could reflect free agency or rational and mature choice on her part, any more than falling in love does. A theme recurring in many of James's works is the control others can exercise over one, not through coercion, but by understanding the vulnerabilities of the very character that is to be lured in a certain direction. Ignorance, error, overwhelming passion, immaturity and inexperience, unconscious motivations that completely reorient a person's objectives in life – these elements are all present in a way that seriously compromises Isabel's capacity for rational choice. These factors, viewed in the law and morals as aberrations and distortions, are viewed by James as characteristic of the human condition. In James's depiction of Isabel, we get explanations of Isabel's behavior that in a more legalistic context would count as excusing conditions, depriving the agent of full accountability. Readers are informed that Isabel initially finds Gilbert appealing as a potential spouse largely out of a sense of guilt for having come undeserved upon so much money. Lavishing it on a man with Gilbert's refined taste and limited means would redeem her anguish. "He would use her fortune in a way that would make her think better of it and rub off a certain grossness attaching to the good luck of an unexpected inheritance" (chapter 42).

Somehow Isabel failed to notice the harsh qualities in Osmond everyone else found manifest. Isabel and Gilbert were initially charmed by one another, and this biased their assessment of one another's character.

Finally, Isabel's loyalty to her choice of a husband is portrayed as the result of an almost all-powerful social given. For Isabel, honor, decency, and responsibility all require that one deals with mistakes by living with their consequences without complaint or public exposure. James is clear that even if one can be said to choose on the basis of one's values, the values themselves are not subject to rational evaluation. So the fact of choice, while not irrelevant, is not morally decisive either.

Isabel treats her hopes for intimate sharing as if they had no standing in her decision making. Ironically, Isabel shares this model of behavior – a thoroughly conventionalist standard – with Gilbert. In the terms of my argument, this reflects a failure to see intimate spheres of her life as having an integrity.

Gilbert's failure to see institutions like marriage as having anything beyond traditional and institutional objectives amounts to his being a person in an attenuated sense. He lacks dimensions of feeling and caring that might permit him to see more in intimate relationships than ironclad rituals for interaction. The difference between Gilbert and Isabel is that she experiences the failures of the relationship as a failure in feelings and connections whereas Gilbert experiences the failure as one of form. Gilbert fears that Isabel does not comply with his explicit demands.[6] His inability to relate intimately with another leaves only self-interest and convention as bases for practical judgment.

How, then, can one tell which spheres can be sacrificed and when? The spheres of a person's life have a voice, a claim. Just as there may be people who are not taken into account in moral and political discourse, there may be parts of selves that are not adequately represented in an individual's life scheme. We structure social life to offer opportunities for those spheres that are recognized in the culture as characteristically indispensable for individuals. We structure social life to respect, to offer scope for these spheres, even if what is promoted within these spheres does not inevitably contribute to the social good. Recognition of the integrity of these spheres becomes part of our ideal conception of social life and of our understanding of a person. It provides the context and opportunity for social freedom.

In this chapter, I have tried to shed some light on the

distinctive moral features of private life. The argument was tied to some literary explorations. By seeing private life in the context of situated human drama, we uncovered several important factors: First, we observed that private life is itself divided into many spheres; second, we observed that each of these spheres can represent an important relationship for the individual and be distinguished by its own character and rules; third, we saw some of what it means to say that a sphere of life has its own integrity; fourth, we went into some detail about the difference between moral judgment in private and in public contexts, pointing out what makes moral judgment in private contexts different from moral judgment generally. We observed that in private spheres, we aim at maintaining relationships with particular, given individuals, whereas in most of our public spheres, individuals are regarded somewhat as abstract place holders or role players who could be replaced without much impact. We noted that morality, as characteristically conceived, maintains structures and institutions, presupposing a paradigm of people as replaceable role players in an essentially impersonal context. This suggests why specific rules, rights, and obligations feature so prominently in moral judgment in the public domain and, similarly, why virtues and wide-ranging discretion operate most prominently in the private realm, where the objective is to maintain relationships and not to achieve impersonal, institutional ends. The private spheres constitute the realm where individuals are to find self-oriented goals, whereas in public life, to a much greater extent, impersonal attitudes are expected.

Epilogue

The main focus of this book has been on the intersection of some topics surprisingly scantily represented in the standard moral philosophy literature: the social and cognitive psychology of human judgment, social freedom, and the general structure of moral judgment in private life. Inquiry in any one of these areas provides counterpoints to some widely accepted principles of moral theory. Their combination suggests that the way philosophers have framed issues for theoretical discussion may obscure rather than clarify some key pieces of the moral picture.

In exploring a role for privacy in the social context, we have come to see it as a means of regulating the amount of social control afforded individuals within associations, both public and private. Trying to understand why both individuals and associations need a social control mechanism like privacy, we came to realize some important truths about both individuals and groups.

About individuals we realized that the sort of independence, cognitive and motivational, that is presupposed in much moral theorizing is radically misguided. The prospect and the desirability of people's coming to a moral stance independent of cultural influence were called into question. The prospect and the desirability of people's forming judgments without reference to what those around them think about the issues and without reference to what others would think about those people were they to disregard the influence of those others came to seem not the humanizing and liberating force so often represented in abstract moral theorizing.

About the group, we realized that to be effective social agents, individuals are, by and large, dependent on groups. To be effective, groups require some social control mechanisms to maintain organization and direction of group life. Groups also require some freedom to pursue objectives and employ methods of their own.

Social freedom, we concluded, did not describe a condition in which individuals are left alone by others. Social freedom, instead, is a condition of having opportunities to pursue with others significant ends without enduring unfair or unreasonable social sacrifices.

Privacy, I argued, must be seen in the context of realistic understandings of how people stand vis-à-vis one another for moral insight. This led us to recognize that life in a group – that is, being a participant in group processes, and being dependent upon groups for socially effective agency – should be made a central element of moral understanding, and certainly a central element of an understanding of freedom. Recognition of how groups, from the intimate to the entire social order, function in life should be incorporated into moral philosophy. Instead, philosophers have tended to parse the social and political world into governments and individuals, with occasional recognition afforded to "the" society as a whole.

Within the discussion of privacy proper, I have differentiated privacy in public life from privacy in private life, and discussed the ends and dynamics of each. Of major concern to me is the connection of privacy with associative dimensions of life. Associations of people, like the individuals who compose the associations, require privacy. Privacy restricted to seclusion of a person from others affords us a glimpse of only a fraction of the role of privacy. And the glimpse is of something uncharacteristic at that, for it highlights the ways we are unconnected with others. Primarily, privacy functions in the context of enabling and facilitating associative features of life, features that in certain stages of history are constitutive of social freedom.

My attempt to show in what ways moral thinking should be reformed to appreciate better the role of privacy has not been, regrettably, as straightforward or as elegant as snapping a rubber band to reform theorizing about identity. Nor would I contend that I represent the only voice in the critical wilderness. I take comfort in recognizing the chorus of critical voices that resonates in me, shaping the thought and style of my effort, and especially in recognizing how much more eloquently and carefully others can and will make the case.

Notes

1 "Rights of Children, Rights of Parents, and the Moral Basis of the Family," *Ethics* 91 (1980), pp. 6–19.
2 For an elegant argument to the effect that rationality admits of no formal or even narrow analysis, see Allan Gibbard, *Wise Choices, Apt Feelings* (Cambridge, Mass.: Harvard University Press, 1990).
3 For an elaborate and elegant argument that economic rationality does a poor job of modeling moral thought, see Michael Slote, *Beyond Optimizing* (Cambridge, Mass.: Harvard University Press, 1989).
4 There is still an important role for moral theories to play. Their role is different from the one that their proponents predicate for them. Let me use an analogy here. Kurt Gödel's incompleteness theorem establishes that there are mathematical truths that are unprovable. It does not show that there are *provable* truths that disciplined mathematicians or Turing machines cannot establish, only that rational proofs have their limits. No one thinks that these limits provide a reason for throwing out notions of rigorous proofs or for questioning the relevance of metatheory, the theory about the nature and limits of logic and mathematics. Indeed, Gödel also showed that, unless a theory of a certain richness and power had these limitations, the theory would be inconsistent. So, too, moral theory may have its limitations recognized without being devalued. Ultimately, like its mathematical counterpart, its limitations may be evidence of its cogency.

1. THE MEANING AND SCOPE OF PRIVACY

1 "Privacy," *Harvard Law Review* 4 (1890), pp. 193–220; reprinted in Ferdinand David Schoeman, ed., *Philosophical Dimensions of Privacy: An Anthology* (Cambridge: Cambridge University Press, 1984), pp. 75–103.

2 *Stanley v. Georgia*, 394 United States 557 (1969), recognizes a right to possess privately pornographic materials in one's home despite legitimate prohibitions on sale or purchase of these materials.

3 *Loving v. Virginia*, 388 United States 1 (1967).

4 *Griswold v. Connecticut*, 381 United States 479 (1965), establishes a married couple's right to obtain and use contraceptives. *Eisenstadt v. Baird*, 405 United States 438 (1972), regards the right to privacy as including the right of unmarried people to use contraceptives. *Carey v. Population Services International*, 431 United States 678 (1977).

5 *Skinner v. Oklahoma*, 317 United States 535 (1942), recognizes a constitutional right to bear children.

6 *Roe v. Wade*, 410 United States 367 (1973), recognizes a woman's right to have an abortion during the first two trimesters of pregnancy as an aspect of her constitutional right to privacy.

7 *Bowers v. Hardwick*, 478 United States 1039 (1986).

8 William Parent, "Recent Work on the Concept of Privacy," *American Philosophical Quarterly* 20 (1983), pp. 341–56, presents a comprehensive analysis and critique of efforts to define privacy, and advocates a narrow view of privacy. It follows from his definition that if everything personal about an individual became publicly documented, there would be no possibility of his *losing* his privacy, even though it would seem as if there would be no possibility of his *having* any.

9 I contrast privacy and autonomy throughout this book. The basic ideal central to standard notions of autonomy is successfully exercising control over one's life and values. Minimally, there must be both intelligence and rationality reflected in the choice as well as a worthwhile range of options to choose among for autonomy to be attributable to a person. For an illuminating account of autonomy, see Joseph Raz, *The Morality of Freedom* (Oxford: Oxford University Press, 1986), chap. 14. There are other accounts of autonomy that characterize a person as being autonomous when she acts in a way that expresses

her deepest moral nature. Such latter theories emphasize the quality of behavior as well as the history of the behavior as the outcome of an uncoerced decision. For such a theory see John Rawls, *A Theory of Justice* (Cambridge, Mass.: Harvard University Press, 1971), p. 515. Finally, there are accounts of autonomy that focus on the character of a person's principles, and her integrity in living up to them, independent of what consequences result for the agent. Thus, according to some, one can exercise one's autonomy serving a prison term or worse for following one's own values. For a critical overview of the many and conflicting directions advocates of autonomy have taken, see Joel Feinberg, *Harm to Self: The Moral Limits of the Criminal Law*, vol. 3 (New York: Oxford University Press, 1986), chap. 17.

10 Catharine A. MacKinnon, "Feminism, Marxism, Method, and the State: Toward Feminist Jurisprudence," *Signs: Journal of Women in Culture and Society* 8 (1983), pp. 635–58.

11 Mary Douglas describes this process in *Purity and Danger: an Analysis of Concepts of Pollution and Taboo* (New York: Praeger, 1966).

12 See David Flaherty, *Privacy in Colonial New England* (Charlottesville: University of Virginia Press, 1972). Many colonial towns, as well as many ancient and modern cultures, required single people to belong to a household.

13 Carol Greenhouse, *Praying for Justice* (Ithaca, N.Y.: Cornell University Press, 1986), p. 48. The Turkish movie *Yol* explores the conflict between family roles and personal or expressive relationships.

14 *The Human Condition* (Chicago: University of Chicago Press, 1958).

15 "Privacy, Freedom, and Respect for Persons," in Ferdinand David Schoeman, ed., *Philosophical Dimensions of Privacy: An Anthology* (Cambridge: Cambridge University Press, 1984), pp. 223–44.

16 "Über Scham und Schamgefühl," in Max Scheler, *Schriften aus dem Nachlass* (Berne: Francke, 1957), pp. 65–147. I am grateful to Eugene Schoeman for painstakingly translating this essay from the German for me.

17 This point is discussed much more extensively in Chapter 10.

18 See John Sabini and Maury Silver, "Emotions, Responsibility, and Character," in Ferdinand David Schoeman, ed., *Respon-*

sibility, Character and the Emotions: New Essays in Moral Psychology (Cambridge: Cambridge University Press, 1987), 165–78.

19 Arlie Hochchild has argued that emotional response, like emotional expression and behavior, is subject to management by a variety of framing and feeling rules. See "Emotion Work, Feeling Rules, and Social Structure," *American Journal of Sociology* 85 (1979), pp. 551–74.

20 Cambridge, Mass.: Harvard University Press, 1984.

21 *Principles of Psychology*, 2: 1049.

22 See Ferdinand David Schoeman, "Privacy and Intimate Information," in Ferdinand David Schoeman, ed., *Philosophical Dimensions of Privacy* (Cambridge: Cambridge University Press, 1984), pp. 403–18.

23 "Make your contribution as informative as is required (for the current purposes of the exchange)." Paul Grice, "Logic and Conversation," in Paul Grice, *Studies in the Way of Words* (Cambridge, Mass.: Harvard University Press, 1989), pp. 1–144.

24 The tort of privacy does focus on social exposure, not governmental or business intervention. Thus most privacy tort scholars focus on the social function of privacy.

25 Some might suspect that rights and wrongs of social control are not discussed because too much is at stake for people in positions of social power to permit these reflections to go unchallenged.

2. MILL'S APPROACH TO SOCIAL FREEDOM

1 John Stuart Mill, *On Liberty*, in A. D. Lindsay, ed., *Utilitarianism, Liberty, and Representative Government* (New York: E. P. Dutton, 1951), pp. 89–90.

2 But there must be more to human nature than rational assessment because Mill's insistence that people forge a life that fits them personally would have little scope were it not that there were individual differences reason could not exhaust.

3 In his *Autobiography* (New York: Columbia University Press, 1924), Mill relates his conviction that, for most of mankind, what is taken for truth must be taken on authority (p. 148): "The mass of mankind, including even their rulers in all the practical departments of life, must, from the necessity of the case, accept most of their opinions on political and social mat-

ters, as they do on physical, from the authority of those who have bestowed more study on those subjects than they generally have it in their power to do." But when talking about the education of his peers, he says (p. 22): "Most boys or youths who have had much knowledge drilled into them, have their mental capacities not strengthened, but overlayed by it. They are crammed with mere facts, and with opinions or phrases of other people, and these are accepted as a substitute for the power to form opinions of their own: and thus the sons of eminent fathers, who have spared no pains in their education, so often grow up mere parroters of what they have learnt, incapable of using their minds except in the furrows traced for them."

4   Mill, *On Liberty*, pp. 91–2. From a reading of Mill's essay on Bentham (*Mill on Bentham and Coleridge* [London: Chatto & Windus, 1950]), one might argue that much of Mill's criticism of Bentham stems from Bentham's disregard of social practices because Bentham could not locate a rationale within utilitarian strictures for them. But that is not Mill's point. Mill is critical of Bentham because he failed to show sensitivity toward the normal range of moral concerns, not because he paid insufficient deference to views that he could not defend.

5   Gilbert Harman, *Change in View* (Cambridge, Mass.: MIT Press, 1986), pp. 38–9: "The foundations theory says people should keep track of their reasons for believing as they do and should stop believing anything that is not associated with adequate evidence.... Furthermore, since people rarely keep track of their reasons, the theory implies that people are unjustified in almost all their beliefs. This is an absurd result!"

6   Mill, *On Liberty*, p. 137.

7   Mill, *On Liberty*, p. 138.

8   Mill, *On Liberty*, pp. 95–6. Emphasis added.

9   Mill, *On Liberty*, p. 178.

10 Mill, *On Liberty*, p. 179. Emphasis added.

11 H. L. A. Hart's "Prolegomenon to Principles of Punishment," in H. L. A. Hart, ed., *Punishment and Responsibility* (Oxford: Oxford University Press, 1968), pp. 1–27.

12 Mill, *On Liberty*, p. 182. The significance of the role of resentment is ably developed in Joel Feinberg, *Harm to Others* (New York: Oxford University Press, 1984), sec. 4.

13 Joel Feinberg's discussion closely follows Mill's principle here.

14 Mill, *On Liberty*, pp. 89–90.

15 See Thomas Kuhn, *Structure of Scientific Revolution* (Chicago: University of Chicago Press, 1962), and Paul Feyerabend, *Against Method* (London: Verso, 1978).

3. ARTICULATED RATIONALITY AND THE
ARCHIMEDEAN CRITIQUE OF CULTURE

1 David Riesman, Reuel Denny, and Nathan Glazer, *The Lonely Crowd: A Study of the Changing American Character* (New Haven: Yale University Press, 1950).

2 Riesman et al., *The Lonely Crowd*, p. 22.

3 Riesman et al., *The Lonely Crowd*, p. 83.

4 Irving Janis, *Groupthink: Psychological Studies of Policy Decisions and Fiascoes* (Boston: Houghton Mifflin, 1982), p. 5.

5 Janis, *Groupthink*, p. 247.

6 Janis, *Groupthink*, p. 12.

7 Janis cites as an example a group of people who came together to quit smoking putting pressure on one of their group who actually succeeded in quitting to begin again because all the others developed the outlook that smoking was not under their control. See Janis, *Groupthink*, p. 8.

8 Lest one think that social norms cannot correct other social norms, think of how people react to racist or sexist jokes. Norms of what is funny or appropriate to laugh at are changed by norms of social justice.

9 I differentiate having a more profound moral understanding and having the motivation or disposition to act accordingly. I am aware that utilitarians have argued that though utilitarianism is the best theory of the right, general awareness of this may not be the best practical route to promoting right behavior. Henry Sidgwick, in *The Methods of Ethics* (New York: Dover, 1966), argues that this is the case, and that it is or may be genuinely frustrating to ethical objectives for people to be aware of the foundations of ethics and second-guess ordinary, generally useful practices. R. M. Hare argues, in *Moral Thinking: Its Levels, Method, and Point* (Oxford: Clarendon Press, 1981), that critical moral thinking must be distinguished from intuitive moral thinking, but that it is impractical for humans actually to engage the critical stance in everyday contexts because of cognitive and motivational limitations. In practice, we

do better to rely on prima facie principles and culturally instilled dispositions than to resort continually to critical analysis. Still, for Hare there is a theoretically correct outlook that
can be elaborated without reference to any particular social
practice or understanding; it is by reference to this outlook
that the prima facie principles and socially instilled dispositions
can be evaluated. It is entirely unconvincing that what really
makes an act or act type right or wrong is the limited range
of considerations that consequentialists recognize.

10 Here I should interject another vision for moral theory. It has
also been suggested that moral theory aims at describing our
moral capacity, analogous to the way theories of grammar aim
at describing our sense of grammar. John Rawls, *A Theory of
Justice* (Cambridge, Mass.: Harvard University Press, 1971),
pp. 46–7.

11 Laurence Thomas, *Living Morally: A Psychology of Moral Character* (Philadelphia: Temple University Press, 1989), p. 15.

12 "An Answer to the Question: What Is Enlightenment?" in I.
Kant, *Perpetual Peace and Other Essays on Politics, History, and
Morals* (Indianapolis: Hackett, 1983), p. 33. Describing himself
as a Kantian, Charles Fried, in "Is Liberty Possible?" in Sterling
McMurrin, ed., *The Tanner Lectures on Human Values*, vol. 3
(Salt Lake City: University of Utah Press, 1982), pp. 94–5, expresses his moral allegiance to independence from cultural
context: "A man is responsible for his own judgments because
they express his moral personality, the exercise of his rational
capacities – they are his. He is responsible for what he becomes
because he chooses a conception of the good and lives according to it. . . . And so in this most basic way we are separate,
even lonely beings, choosing alone and responsible as we
choose."

13 *The Savage Mind* (Chicago: University of Chicago Press, 1966),
pp. 13–14.

14 Cambridge, Mass.: Harvard University Press, 1971.

15 Of course, it is true that reflective equilibrium does provide
an anchor to keep us from drifting morally or, to switch the
metaphor, a rudder to guide us sensibly in the search for
fundamental principles of social organization.

16 Rawls does argue (in *A Theory of Justice*, chap. 8) that being
brought up in a just society has a major structural impact on
one's moral psychology, but he uses this discussion to establish

the stability of the just society through an understanding of the incentives to identify with, or internalize, principles of justice.

17 Rawls, *A Theory of Justice*, p. 256.
18 This aspect of contract theory is clearly presented in David Gauthier's treatment of morality in *Morals by Agreement* (New York: Oxford University Press, 1986).
19 Jon Elster, *The Cement of Society: A Study of Social Order* (Cambridge: Cambridge University Press, 1989), p. 36.
20 Annette Baier, "Trust and Antitrust," *Ethics* 96 (1986), pp. 231–60.
21 Baier, "Trust and Antitrust," p. 240.
22 This is true of contractarian and utilitarian theories, the latter having given rise to welfare economics and social choice theory, which define rationality in terms of efficiency.
23 Ronald Dworkin, "Lord Devlin and the Enforcement of Morals," *Yale Law Journal* 75 (1966), pp. 987–1105.
24 Dworkin, "Lord Devlin...," p. 999.
25 Dworkin, "Lord Devlin...," p. 997.
26 As, for instance, represented in his book, *Law's Empire* (Cambridge, Mass.: Harvard University Press, 1985).
27 Ronald Dworkin, "Liberal Community," *California Law Review* 77 (1989), pp. 479–504.
28 Jeremy Waldron, "Particular Values and Critical Morality," *California Law Review* 77 (1989), pp. 561–89.
29 Waldron, "Particular Values...," p. 577.
30 *A Theory of the Right and the Good* (Oxford: Oxford University Press, 1979), pp. 21–2.

4. SOCIAL FREEDOM FROM THE PERSPECTIVE OF COGNITIVE AND SOCIAL PSYCHOLOGY

1 Quoting from the *Restatement of the Law, Second, Torts 2d*, vol. 2 (St. Paul, Minn.: American Law Institute 1965); sec. 283, p. 12, "Qualities of the 'reasonable man.'... The fact that this judgment is personified in a 'man' calls attention to the necessity of taking into account the fallibility of human behavior."
2 Amos Tversky and Daniel Kahneman, "Judgment under Uncertainty: Heuristics and Biases," in Daniel Kahneman, Paul Slovic, and Amos Tversky, eds., *Judgment under Uncertainty:*

Heuristics and Biases (Cambridge: Cambridge University Press, 1982), p. 14.

3 Elizabeth Loftus, *Eyewitness Testimony* (Cambridge, Mass.: Harvard University Press, 1979), and *Eyewitness Testimony: Civil and Criminal* (New York: Kluwer Law Book Publishers, 1987).

4 Muzafer Sherif, "Group Influences upon the Formation of Norms and Attitudes," in T. Newcomb and E. Hartley, eds., *Readings in Social Psychology* (New York: Henry Holt, 1947), pp. 77–89.

5 Morton Deutsch and Harold Gerard, "A Study of Normative and Informational Social Influences upon Individual Judgment," *Journal of Abnormal and Social Psychology* 36 (1955), pp. 311–37.

6 Solomon Asch, "Studies of Independence and Conformity: I. A Minority of One against a Unanimous Majority," *Psychological Monographs: General and Applied* 70, no. 9 (1956), pp. 1–70.

7 John Sabini and Maury Silver, *Moralities of Everyday Life* (Oxford: Oxford University Press, 1982), pp. 84–5.

8 Solomon Asch, *Social Psychology* (Englewood Cliffs, N.J.: Prentice-Hall, 1952), p. 457.

9 In a series of further studies that were variations on Asch's experimental setup, Morton Deutsch and Harold Gerard showed that various factors had an impact on the degree to which subjects conformed to the majority judgment when they had reason to think it wrong. They found that the extent to which people felt that they and others were part of a group increased tendencies to conform, but also that it was possible for groups to instill a high degree of independent assessment in its members. See "A Study of Normative and Informational Social Influences upon Individual Judgment," *Journal of Abnormal and Social Psychology* 51 (1955), pp. 629–36.

10 Stanley Milgram, *Obedience to Authority* (New York: Harper & Row, 1974).

11 R. Nisbett and T. Wilson, "Telling More Than We Can Know: Verbal Reports on Mental Processes," *Psychological Review* 84 (1977), pp. 231–59.

12 Bibb Latanè and John Darley, *The Unresponsive Bystander: Why Doesn't He Help?* (New York: Appleton-Century-Crofts, 1970).

13 Harvey Hornstein, E. Fisch, and M. Holmes, "Influence of a Model's Feelings about His Behavior and His Relevance as a

Comparison Other on Observers' Helping Behavior," *Journal of Personality and Social Psychology* 10 (1968), pp. 222–6.

14 P. Zimbardo, "The Mind Is a Formidable Jailer: A Pirandellian Prisoner," *New York Times Magazine*, April 8, 1973. For a discussion of this study, see Sabini and Silver, *Moralities of Everyday Life*, chap. 4.

15 Zimbardo, "The Mind Is a Formidable Jailer . . . ," pp. 56–7.

16 Nisbett and Wilson, "Telling More Than We Can Know . . . ," p. 248.

17 This question is pursued in detail in Ferdinand David Schoeman, "Statistical Norms and Moral Attributions," in Ferdinand David Schoeman, ed., *Responsibility, Character and the Emotions: New Studies in Moral Psychology* (New York: Cambridge University Press, 1987), pp. 287–315.

18 The *Restatement of the Law, Second Torts 2d*, vol. 2, p. 11, in characterizing the appropriate standard of conduct as discovered in tort law, says: "Therefore it does not include acts which, although done with every precaution which it is practicable to demand, involve an irreducible minimum of danger to others, but which are so far justified by their utility or traditional usage that even the most perfect system of preventive law would not forbid them."

19 Dale Miller and Cathy McFarland, "Counterfactual Thinking and Victim Compensation: A Test of Norm Theory," *Personality and Social Psychology Bulletin* 12 (1986), pp. 513–19.

20 Dale Miller and S. Gunasegaram, "Temporal Order and the Perceived Mutability of Events," in D. Miller, W. Turnbull, and C. McFarland, "Counterfactual Thinking and Social Perception: Thinking about What Might Have Been," in M. P. Zanna, ed., *Advances in Experimental Social Psychology*, vol. 23 (Orlando, Fla.: Academic Press, 1990), pp. 305–32.

21 Daniel Kahneman and Dale Miller, in "Norm Theory: Comparing Reality to Its Alternatives," *Psychological Review* 93 (1986), pp. 136–53.

22 Miller and McFarland, "Counterfactual Thinking . . . ," p. 517.

23 Kahneman and Miller, "Norm Theory . . . ," p. 146.

24 Cathaleene Jones and Elliot Aronson, "Attribution of Fault to a Rape Victim as a Function of Respectability of the Victim," *Journal of Personality and Social Psychology* 26 (1973), pp. 415–19.

25 I am indebted to Owen Flanagan's book *Varieties of Moral Ex-*

perience (Cambridge, Mass.: Harvard University Press, 1990) for emphasizing some of the problems of drawing general inferences from localized research.

5. THE IMPORTANCE OF CULTURAL AUTHORITY FOR MORALITY

1   Edna Ullmann-Margalit, in her illuminating book *The Emergence of Norms* (Oxford: Oxford University Press, 1977), chap. 3, sec. 2.3, characterizes conformism as a misguided personal tendency to deal with noncoordination problems as if they were coordination problems. She argues that all norms can be conceived as resulting from solutions to three sorts of social phenomena: prisoner's dilemma, coordination, and inequality.

As I argue in this book, this conceptualization is inadequate. First of all our tendencies to conform may be functional in maintaining social cohesiveness and social caring outside of contexts of coordination, maintaining inequality, and prisoner's dilemma problems. So while we take it for granted that diverse cultures prescribe diverse codes for dressing, there is little plausibility in thinking that how we dress individually or communally responds to the sort of problems Ullmann-Margalit addresses and thinks adequately exhaustive. She does not see or allow for mere identification with others as a basis for norm emergence, and prefers to analyze norms in terms of self-interest. I argue that in addition to coordination, we also benefit from participation and involvement with others, and that these sorts of benefits are not the sort characterized by achieving equilibriums, except in a trivial sense. If our goal is to meet, we require coordination. If our goal is to speak, we require conventions for speech. If our goal, however, is to stay warm, there is no analogous reason why your patterns of dress should affect mine, though clearly they do. The reason to dress like others and more generally to live life like others I suggest is grounded in reasons besides those cataloged by Ullmann-Margalit.

Let us try to be clear about the differences. I am claiming that group identification and conformity is advantageous for people, but that this is not so in the way normally characterized by coordination problems. But it seems that if I say that people (individually) are better off doing A_1 rather than A_2 provided others do A_1, and that they are better off doing A_2 rather than A_1 provided others do A_2, doesn't this just fit right in with the classic conditions for coordination? If people are genuinely better off conforming, then conforming is just classic coordination.

In response, I suggested that if driving on the right or meeting is taken as the characteristic picture of coordination, then practices like dress or religious belief do not fit. If the focus of dressing is staying warm and if the focus of religious belief is communion with God, then what others do seems irrelevant in ways that driving on the right or meeting at the biggest station do not. And it is for such sorts of behavior that we find conformity and that I look for a rationale. If we have an inherent need to be like others, then satisfying this need presents us with a standard coordination problem. But the point is that the end in view is characteristically local for classic coordination problems and global for the sorts of patterns that concern me. The notion of being "better off" is ambiguous. A person who had only selfish motivations or who was sociopathic might not recognize that he would be better off were he to care more about others. The element of judgment is taken out of the decision problem by construing the agent's judgment as the appropriately guiding one. Whereas *we* might say that a selfish person is an emotional cripple who would be better off were he different, he would not see it this way, and would thus make his choices accordingly. Because decision theory aspires to explain just the sort of norms I am here invoking, these norms are treated as unavailable until selfishly rationalized.

The apparatus of norm reconstruction that guides decision theorists is methodologically individualistic, admittedly positing self-interested agents. So classic discussions of coordination problems do not explicitly raise questions of group loyalty and group identification as motivating. It is not the formal structure of coordination strategies that is hostile to treating social concern as relevant, but the strictures of application on the part of those who develop the theory. Similar reservations will arise when I discuss some of Jon Elster's views.

2 Bell's Inequality is a test by which physicists differentiate the possibility of a classical, though hidden, explanation of micro-

phenomena and nonclassical or quantum-mechanical phenomena. The Banach-Tarski Theorem establishes that any two similarly shaped objects with at least three dimensions can be decomposed into a *finite* number of parts that are congruent.

3 Here I am not assuming that law does not embody moral principles. I am only assuming that there can be a conflict between what a judge treats as judicially required, all things considered, and what the judge thinks is morally right.

4 Solomon Asch, "Issues in the Study of Social Influences on Judgment," in Irwin Berg and Bernard Bass, eds., *Conformity and Deviation* (New York: Harper & Brothers, 1961), pp. 143–58.

5 Quoting from *Prosser and Keeton on The Law of Torts*, 5th ed. (St. Paul Minn.: West, 1984), p. 193: "Since the standard is a community standard, evidence of the usual and customary conduct of others under similar circumstances is normally relevant and admissible, as an indication of what the community regards as proper, and a composite judgment as to the risks of the situation and the precautions required to meet them. Custom also bears upon what others will expect the actor to do, and what, therefore, reasonable care may require the actor to do, upon the feasibility of taking precautions, the difficulty of change, and the actor's opportunity to learn the risks and what is called for to meet them. If the actor does only what everyone else has done, there is at least an inference that the actor is conforming to the community's idea of reasonable behavior.... [C]ustoms and usages themselves are many and various; some are the result of careful thought and decision, while others arise from the kind of inadvertence, carelessness, indifference, cost-paring and corner-cutting that normally is associated with negligence.... It follows that where common knowledge and ordinary judgment will recognize unreasonable danger, what everyone does may be found to be negligent."

6 See also Daniel Dennett, "The Moral First Aid Manual," in Sterling McMurrin, ed., *The Tanner Lectures on Human Values*, Vol. 8 (Salt Lake City: University of Utah Press, 1988), pp. 119–47.

7 The exhibit of the Ice Age communities at the New York Natural History Museum beautifully illustrates this claim.

8 I suspect that there is a very limited cultural context in which the objective of success is among those objectives parents seek for their children.

9 Some of the goods it promotes may be part of a functional explanation of why members of our species are directed toward such ends. But as several writers have recently pointed out, explanation on a biological level is not at all the same as motivation on an individual level. See Laurence Thomas, *Living Morally: A Psychology of Moral Character* (Philadelphia: Temple University Press, 1989), and Allan Gibbard, *Wise Choices, Apt Feelings* (Cambridge, Mass.: Harvard University Press, 1990).

10 Couldn't utilitarians agree with this criticism of other moral positions and be themselves immune to it? No, for two reasons. First, the individual and the social good are not related in the right way within utilitarian theory. For the utilitarian, a life shared with others is not sought because it is a social good, and is not a good because it is a social good. A social good, for the utilitarian, is a methodological construct comprising the individual goods of individuals. Its value is constructive and derivative. Second, the objective of social good for the utilitarian is not a life shared with others for its own sake, even though the latter could be seen as a social good.

Well, then, am I saying that life in community with others would be good even if it were not good for the individuals involved? Here I would offer the response that the enterprise of evaluating good for an individual is too closely and internally tied to make sense of the suggested alternative. I will admit though that a being could be born of humans who had no social nature and for whom social life is no good. Severely and thoroughly autistic people are examples. But they also illustrate our tragic difficulty in admitting them as persons in the first place, establishing a conceptual connection between being a person and being socially engaged.

11 Annette Baier, "Trust and Antitrust," *Ethics* 96 (1986), p. 243.

12 Donald Campbell, "On the Conflicts between Biological and Social Evolution and between Psychology and Moral Tradition," *American Psychologist* 30 (1975), pp. 1003–1126.

13 Gibbard, *Wise Choices, Apt Feelings*, pp. 64–9. In general I would highly commend Gibbard's book for, among other virtues, its recognition of a role for extrarational tendencies in humans.

14 This is the dominant theme in David Gauthier's influential *Morals by Agreement* (Oxford: Clarendon Press, 1985).

15 Clifford Geertz, "The Growth of Culture and the Evolution of Mind," in Clifford Geertz, *The Interpretation of Cultures: Selected Essays* (New York: Basic Books, 1971), pp. 82–3.

16 "The Impact of the Concept of Culture on the Concept of Man," and "The Growth of Culture and the Evolution of Mind," in Geertz, *The Interpretation of Cultures: Selected Essays*, pp. 33–54 and 55–83.

17 Geertz, "The Growth of Culture . . . ," pp. 68–9.

18 Geertz, "The Growth of Culture . . . ," p. 83.

19 Joseph Raz, "Legitimate Authority," in *The Authority of Law* (Oxford: Oxford University Press, 1979), esp. pp. 18–27. Quoted from p. 27. In considering issues in this section, I also benefited from Raz's discussion of authority in *The Morality of Freedom* (Oxford: Oxford University Press, 1986), chaps. 2–4.

20 This too is the position of Raz, *Morality of Freedom*.

21 If we consider the religious domain as important for people even though not exhausted by reference to reasons that would be independently found valid, then we have an example of an authority for people that violates Raz's requirement. Although some may think that religion provides incentives to be moral and may be a way to eternal bliss – reasons people have to act independent of religious motivation – many practitioners would think that restriction to such reasons is a misleading picture of religious outlooks, and exemplifies the impoverishment of philosophical imperialism.

22 Gibbard, in *Wise Choices, Apt Feelings*, offers the advantages of coordination as an evolutionary basis explaining the susceptibility to others' influence.

23 Raz, *Morality of Freedom*, p. 53, claims this to be the proper justification of all authority. Raz accepts what he calls the "normal justification thesis," according to which "the normal way to establish that a person has authority over another person involves showing that the alleged subject is likely better to comply with reasons which apply to him (other than the alleged authoritative directives) if he accepts the directives of the alleged authority as authoritatively binding and tries to follow them, rather than by trying to follow the reasons which apply to him directly."

24 Raz, *Morality of Freedom*, p. 29.
25 See Hilary Putnam, "Why Reason Can't be Naturalized," *Synthese* 52 (1982), pp. 3–24, esp. p. 14.
26 John Holland, Keith Holyoak, Richard Nisbett, and Paul Thagard, in *Induction: Processes of Inference, Learning, and Discovery* (Cambridge, Mass.: MIT Press, 1986), argue that this flexibility and competition among conflicting rules is central to nearly all reasoning. Sabina Lovibond, in *Realism and Imagination in Ethics* (Oxford: Blackwell, 1983), uses the notion of *semantic depth* to explore the possibility of there being moral richness within a concept or institution that goes beyond the individual or conventional limits of understanding at a given time. She also devotes a substantial portion of her book to arguing that conventionalism does not require conservatism.
27 Annette Baier, in her essay "Theory and Reflective Practice," in *Postures of the Mind: Essays on Mind and Morals* (Minneapolis: University of Minnesota Press, 1985), pp. 207–27, elaborates this position.
28 See Thomas S. Kuhn, "Scientific Development and Lexical Change," The Thalheimer Lectures, delivered at the Johns Hopkins University, November 1984. Kuhn points out that the approach to knowledge that we learn from the history of science is that we concentrate on what justifies *changes* in the body of scientific theory.
29 Imagine how much less satisfactory Mill's arguments in favor of liberty of women's equality would have seemed had he restricted himself to utilitarian considerations.
30 Recall the quote in Chapter 3 from Jeremy Waldron where he dismisses any discussion of morality that does not begin and end with equality of moral worth of each individual as out of moral bounds, unworthy of consideration.
31 Norman Daniels, "Equal Liberty and Unequal Worth of Liberty," in Norman Daniels, ed., *Reading Rawls: Critical Studies of a Theory of Justice* (New York: Basic Books, 1975), pp. 253–82.
32 Recently, the presumption of liberty as an independent ideal has been called into question. See Raz, *Morality of Freedom*, pp. 8–12.
33 Deborah Rhode, *Justice and Gender: Sex Discrimination and the Law* (Cambridge, Mass.: Harvard University Press, 1989), pp. 148–9.

34 Rhode, *Justice and Gender*, chap. 5.

35 Laura Nader, "Subordination of Women in Comparative Perspective," *Urban Anthropology and Studies of Cultural Systems* 15 (1986), pp. 377–97.

36 See Ronald Dworkin, *Law's Empire* (Cambridge, Mass.: Harvard University Press, 1986), chap. 2.

37 Edna Ullmann-Margalit, "Revision of Norms," *Ethics* 100 (1990), pp. 756–67.

38 See *Ethics and the Limits of Philosophy* (Cambridge, Mass.: Harvard University Press, 1985). Annette Baier argues a similar position in her paper "Theory and Reflective Practice," as does Martha Craven Nussbaum in "Flawed Crystals: James's *The Golden Bowl* and Literature as Moral Philosophy," *New Literary History* 15 (1983), pp. 25–50, and *The Fragility of Goodness* (Cambridge: Cambridge University Press, 1986). Charles Stevenson also points to the blinding effects of definitions of the good. Stevenson argues that considerations relevant to resolving conflict are of the greatest variety, and that restrictions imposed by definition or theory impoverish the tools we have to deal intelligently with conflict. See his "Emotive Conception of Ethics and Its Cognitive Implications," in *Facts and Values* (New Haven: Yale University Press, 1963), p. 61.

39 Daniel Kahneman and Dale Miller, in "Norm Theory: Comparing Reality to Its Alternatives," *Psychological Review* 93 (1986), pp. 136–53, explore in depth the ways in which we classify and thereby call into operation norms by which we assess what we experience. The authors show the factors leading to the variability of which norms are called into operation by an incident. Whether an event is regarded as normal is influenced by the ease with which an alternative can be imagined. Events we think of as abnormal are ones that readily evoke alternatives. According to "norm theory," judgments of normality differ from judgments of probability. Judgments of probability are independent of the particular evoking experience, whereas judgments of normality depend on what categories the stimulus evokes. See also Dale Miller and Cathy McFarland, "Counterfactual Thinking and Victim Compensation: A Test of Norm Theory," *Personality and Social Psychology Bulletin* 12 (1986), pp. 513–19. See discussion of norm theory in Chapter 4.

40 Claude Steele, "The Psychology of Self-Affirmation: Sustaining

the Integrity of the Self," in Leonard Berkowitz, ed., *Advances in Experimental Social Psychology*, Vol. 21: *Social Psychological Studies of the Self: Perspective and Program* (New York: Academic Press, 1988), p. 279.

41 Steele, "The Psychology of Self-Affirmation . . . ," p. 281.
42 Steele, "The Psychology of Self-Affirmation . . . ," p. 282.
43 Steele, "The Psychology of Self-Affirmation . . . ," pp. 298–9.
44 Constitutional theorists may frame or claim to find principles implicit in the practice that were not formally recognized. But displaying these and expecting the assent of recognition by others is quite a different activity from formulating a theory.
45 As Michael Slote put it in a personal communication, "the 'task' of growing up is to replace total dependence with interdependence," not independence.

6. EXPLAINING PRIVACY'S PLACE

1 Quoting from Erving Goffman's essay, "Fun in Games," in Erving Goffman, *Encounters: Two Studies in the Sociology of Interaction* (Indianapolis: Bobbs-Merrill, 1961), pp. 80–1: "The process of mutually sustaining a definition of the situation in face-to-face interaction is socially organized through rules of relevance and irrelevance. These rules for the management of engrossment appear to be an insubstantial element of social life, a matter of courtesy, manners, and etiquette. But it is to these flimsy rules, and not to the unshaking character of the external world, that we owe our unshaking sense of realities."
2 And if that message is not clear enough, we have only to look to the current generation of socially, emotionally, and educationally deprived youths to see what a decent or stable life requires. Like children who were not exposed to language early enough, these people have missed, maybe irretrievably, the social ties and sense of belonging and caring that goes with these ties. The problem for these people is not a failure in logic.
3 Recall our discussion of first-order and second-order reasons in Chapter 5.
4 See Daniel Kahneman, Jack Knetch, and Richard Thaler, "Fairness as a Constraint on Profit Seeking: Entitlements in the Market," *American Economic Review* 76 (1986), pp. 728–41, and

"Fairness and the Assumptions of Economics," *Journal of Business* 59 (1986), pp. 285–300.

5 Of course many moral philosophers do reject theoretical reconstructions of moral life.

6 A very small percentage of the experimental studies were reviewed in Chapter 4.

7 For an elegant elaboration of how a cultural tradition frames moral questions and issues, see Herbert Fingarette, "Reason, Spontaneity, and the Li – A Confucian Critique of Graham's Solution to the Problem of Fact and Value," in Henry Rosemont, Jr., *Chinese Texts and Philosophical Contexts* (Lasalle: Open Court, 1991), pp. 209–25. See also his paper, "How the Analects Portrays the Ideal of Efficacious Authority," *Journal of Chinese Philosophy* 8 (1981), pp. 29–50.

8 See my discussion of framing effects in Chapter 4.

9 *Brothers and Keepers* (New York: Holt, Rinehart, & Winston, 1984). Similar themes are explored in the film, *Do the Right Thing*, directed by Spike Lee.

10 This is explicitly stressed in John Rawls, *A Theory of Justice* (Cambridge, Mass.: Harvard University Press, 1971), and in David Gauthier, *Morals by Agreement* (New York: Oxford University Press, 1986).

11 George Herbert Mead, *Mind, Self and Society from the Standpoint of a Social Behaviorist* (Chicago: University of Chicago Press, 1934), p. 253.

12 Mead, *Mind, Self and Society*, p. 255.

13 David Daube has speculated that politically differentiated social organizations employ guilt as a means of social control whereas less structured associations use shame. See "The Culture of Deuteronomy," *ORITA* 3 (1969), pp. 27–52.

14 Allan Gibbard elegantly shows the functional role of being subject to social pressures. He argues that this tendency addresses coordination problems that have to be solved. We have to be aware that offering a functional explanation is not the same as offering either a psychological explanation or a justification of the tendency. See Gibbard, *Wise Choices, Apt Feelings* (Cambridge, Mass.: Harvard University Press, 1990).

15 Georg Simmel, *The Sociology of Georg Simmel*, ed. Kurt Wolff (New York: Free Press, 1950), pp. 120–2.

16 A mountain of literature is erupting on strategies to take into account our cognitive, volitional, and emotional shortcomings.

Jon Elster, author of *Sour Grapes* (Cambridge: Cambridge University Press, 1983), and *Ulysses and the Sirens* (Cambridge: Cambridge University Press, 1984), and Thomas Schelling, author of *Micromotives and Macrobehavior* (New York: Norton, 1978), are but two frequent contributors to this literature.

17 John Sabini and Maury Silver, *Moralities of Everyday Life* (New York: Oxford University Press, 1982).

18 Recall here my discussion of Joseph Raz's treatment of authority in Chapter 5. See Joseph Raz, "Legitimate Authority," in *The Authority of Law* (Oxford: Oxford University Press, 1979), pp. 3–27.

19 See Jon Elster, "The Possibility of Rational Politics," in *Solomonic Judgments: Studies in the Limitations of Rationality* (Cambridge: Cambridge University Press, 1989), sec. IV.4.

20 Thomas Schelling has spent a career in discussing accommodations we should make to our personal irrationalities.

21 Gerald Dworkin makes this distinction in his influential essay, "Paternalism," in Richard Wasserstrom, ed., *Morality and the Law* (Belmont: Wadsworth, 1971), pp. 107–26.

22 Because Joel Feinberg defends the Millian principle in general in his multivolume *The Moral Limit of the Criminal Law* (New York: Oxford University Press, 1984–8), and Mill's account of moral emotions in the first volume, *Harm to Others*, this criticism also applies to his analysis. Although Feinberg is almost strictly concerned with legal sanctions, his talk of moral emotions of resentment follows Mill very closely and thus my remarks are applicable to Feinberg as well. For instance, on p. 149, Feinberg compares feeling indignant because another is pompous and being indignant because another has failed to save one's drowning child, when it would have involved no effort or risk to do so. Feinberg argues that we have no right to a person being different in the first respect, but we do in the second, and that this is the basis of legitimacy of the feelings in the second case, though not the first.

23 Not all threats that are rightful fail to count as coercion, as is evidenced in legal coercion's centrality to the criminal law. See Alan Wertheimer, *Coercion* (Princeton: Princeton University Press, 1987). See also Herbert Fingarette, "Victimization, a Legalist Analysis of Coercion, Deception, Undue Influence, and Excusable Prison Escape," *Washington and Lee Law Review*

42 (1985), pp. 65–118. The examples in this paragraph come from Wertheimer.

24 Carol Greenhouse, *Praying for Justice* (Ithaca, N.Y.: Cornell University Press, 1986).

25 Richard Burgh has objected to my claims here by suggesting that if true, they undermine my arguments against moral theory. His concern is that I treat as an abstract and universal principle the position that control that is not required for viability is illegitimate. I wish to observe that adhering to such a principle is not the same as holding a theory. A moral outlook is a theory if it aspires to a deductive structure and orders considerations that may conflict. In disavowing theory one does not have to deny general principles of judgment, but only deny their systematic relationship.

26 Simmel, *Sociology of Georg Simmel*, pp. 416–17.

27 Stanley Schachter, *The Psychology of Affiliation: Experimental Studies of the Sources of Gregariousness* (Stanford, Calif.: Stanford University Press, 1959).

28 In "Role Distance," in Erving Goffman, *Encounters: Two Studies in the Sociology of Interaction* (Indianapolis: Bobbs-Merrill, 1961), p. 101, Goffman describes people in transition between all-encompassing roles or status and those whose relationships are nearly fully differentiated: "There are, for example, ancient inbred island communities of Britain where kinship and fellow-islander status is so fundamental that a native who is employed in a local shop to sell to members of the community is unlikely to build this work activity into a stance to be taken to customers. Such clerks take the point of view of the other not only in manner, as in the case of urban sellers, but as a kinsman, as a neighbor, or as a friend. Often, no variation can be observed in tone or manner as the clerk weaves personal gossipy conversation in amongst the words of advice he offers as to which of the local shops (not just his own) sells which product at the most advantageous price. Here, the richness of communal life entails an impoverishment of the self-defining aspects of occupational roles: required tasks are done, but they are scarcely allowed to form the base for the development of special loyalty and a special orientation to the world. Here doing is not being."

29 Quoting Simmel, *Sociology of Georg Simmel*, pp. 367–8: "In prac-

tice, sociological autonomy presents itself as group egoism: the group pursued its own purposes with the same inconsiderateness for all purposes outside itself which, in the case of the individual, is precisely called egoism. Usually, to be sure, this inconsiderateness is morally justified in the consciousness of the individual members by the fact that the group purposes themselves have a super-individual, objective character; that it is often impossible to name any particular individual who profits from the group's egoistic behavior; and that, as a matter of fact, this behavior often requires the group members' selflessness and sacrifice. But the point here is not to make any ethical valuation, but only to stress the group separation from its environment, which is brought about or characterized by the egoism of the group."

30 Simmel, *Sociology of Georg Simmel*, pp. 360–3.
31 Whether the cultural processes that enhance individuality and privacy represent progress or not can be debated. Some theorists, like Georg Simmel, detect in this differentiation and specialization process a despiritualization of humanity. See Simmel, *Sociology of Georg Simmel*, pp. 421–2.
32 Simmel, *Sociology of Georg Simmel*, pp. 317–18.
33 Simmel, *Sociology of Georg Simmel*, p. 337, advances the view that the private–public distinction in its current, normative sense, is the direct result of cultural differentiation.
34 See Ruth Gavison, "Privacy and the Limits of Law," and Robert Murphy, "Social Distance and the Veil," both reprinted in Ferdinand David Schoeman, ed., *Philosophical Dimensions of Privacy: An Anthology* (Cambridge: Cambridge University Press, 1984), pp. 346–402.

7. THE ASCENT OF PRIVACY

1 Whether it is experienced as an individual concern in contexts where it is not a social practice is something we can be less confident about. I do address this issue in the later parts of this chapter.
2 *The Human Condition* (Chicago: University of Chicago Press, 1958).
3 For the examples in this paragraph, see Paul Veyne, "The Roman Empire," in Philippe Aries and Georges Duby, eds.,

A History of Private Life, Vol. 1: *From Pagan Rome to Byzantium* (Cambridge, Mass.: Harvard University Press, 1987), pp. 163–71.

4 Peter Brown, "Late Antiquity," in Philippe Aries and Georges Duby, eds., *A History of Private Life*, Vol. 1: *From Pagan Rome to Byzantium* (Cambridge, Mass.: Harvard University Press, 1987), p. 261.

5 "Solitude: Eleventh to Thirteenth Century," in Philippe Aries and Georges Duby, eds., *A History of Private Life*, Vol. 2: *Revelations of the Medieval World* (Cambridge, Mass.: Harvard University Press, 1988), p. 510.

6 Brown, "Late Antiquity," pp. 260–2.

7 I am indebted to Professor Martin Donougho for directing me to Elias's work.

8 *The Civilizing Process*, Vol. 1: *History of Manners* (New York: Urizen Books, 1978), pp. 177–8.

9 I am indebted to Ruth Gavison for this observation.

10 *The Civilizing Process*, Vol. 2: *Power and Civility* (New York: Pantheon Books, 1982), p. 241.

11 Michael Rouche, "Early Middle Ages in the West," in Philippe Aries and Georges Duby, eds., *A History of Private Life*, Vol. 1: *From Pagan Rome to Byzantium* (Cambridge, Mass.: Harvard University Press, 1987), pp. 537–45.

12 Duby, "Solitude: Eleventh to Thirteenth Century," pp. 509–33.

13 Philippe Braunstein, "Toward Intimacy: The Fourteenth and Fifteenth Centuries," in Philippe Aries and Georges Duby, eds., *A History of Private Life*, Vol. 2: *Revelations of the Medieval World* (Cambridge, Mass.: Harvard University Press, 1988), pp. 549–54.

14 The main source of these comments is Lawrence Stone's study of English family life in the early modern period, *The Family, Sex and Marriage in England, 1500–1800* (New York: Harper & Row, 1977).

15 Stone, *Family*, p. 4.

16 Stone, *Family*, p. 99.

17 Stone, *Family*, p. 101.

18 Stone, *Family*, p. 101.

19 Stone, *Family*, p. 103.

20 Stone, *Family*, p. 117.

21 Stone, *Family*, p. 93.
22 *Privacy in Colonial New England* (Charlottesville: University of Virginia Press, 1972).
23 Stone, *Family*, p. 635.
24 Stone, *Family*, p. 531.
25 Stone, *Family*, p. 258.
26 Stone, *Family*, p. 202.
27 Stone, *Family*, p. 397.
28 Ian Watt, *The Rise of the Novel* (Berkeley: University of California Press, 1957), p. 148.
29 Watt, *Rise of the Novel*, p. 185.
30 It is worth mentioning that not everyone celebrated this self-conception of person as a role player; Rousseau continually decried new socialization of man as something that made him nothing for himself, empty at the core. Rousseau's opposition was not motivated by a conservative wish for the domination of status, but by an understanding of human nature that flourished in the context of simplicity, self-knowledge, and the courage to be socially what one was privately.
31 Watt, *Rise of the Novel*, p. 13.
32 Lionel Trilling, *Sincerity and Authenticity* (Cambridge, Mass.: Harvard University Press, 1971).
33 Trilling, *Sincerity and Authenticity*, p. 24.
34 Trilling, *Sincerity and Authenticity*, p. 25.
35 Stone, *Family*, p. 216.
36 For a fascinating study of this phenomenon and its significance for Western thought, see Yirmiahu Yovel, *The Marrano of Reason* (Princeton: Princeton University Press, 1989).
37 Watt, *Rise of the Novel*, p. 74.
38 Watt, *Rise of the Novel*, p. 75.
39 See Denis Diderot's *Rameau's Nephew* for expression of this around the year 1760. In a Hassidic tale, a man expresses his experiences upon appearing at heaven's gate. There the angels ask this man not why he did not live up to the standards of a Moses or Jeremiah, but why he did not live up to the standards his own nature imposed.

8. PRIVACY AND GOSSIP

1 Hannah Arendt, "On Humanity in Dark Times," in *Men in Dark Times* (New York: Harcourt, Brace & World, 1968), p. 138,

quoted in Patricia Meyer Spacks, *Gossip* (Chicago: University of Chicago Press, 1985), p. 43.

2   *The Florida Star v. B.J.F.* 109, S. Ct. 2603, 1989.

3   For an illuminating discussion of the different senses to the public–private distinction, as well as of the importance of maintaining the private realm as private, see Ruth Gavison, "The Private–Public Distinction: Why the (Feminist) Invitation to Abolish It Should Be Declined," manuscript dated February 11, 1991.

4   See the discussion of Oliver Sipple early in the next chapter for a tragic case of a person losing control over what is said about him in print once he becomes a "public figure."

5   For an extensive argument about why privacy norms cannot be seen as constitutionally limiting communication in mass media without undermining the First Amendment, see Diane Zimmerman, "Requiem for a Heavyweight: A Farewell to Warren and Brandeis's Privacy Tort," *Cornell Law Review* 68 (1983), pp. 292–367.

6   See Ruth Gavison, "Privacy and the Limits of the Law," in Ferdinand David Schoeman, ed., *Philosophical Dimensions of Privacy* (Cambridge:Cambridge University Press,1984),pp. 346–402.

7   Ruth Gavison's work on privacy emphasizes this contribution of privacy, as have her personal comments on earlier versions of my work. See Gavison, "Privacy and the Limits of the Law," and also "Privacy and the First Amendment," *South Carolina Law Review* 43, no. 3 (1992).

8   "Privacy and Intimate Information," in Ferdinand David Schoeman, ed., *Philosophical Dimensions of Privacy* (Cambridge: Cambridge University Press, 1984), pp. 403–18.

9   Max Gluckman, "Gossip and Scandal," *Current Anthropology* 4 (1963), pp. 307–16.

10   John Sabini and Maury Silver, "Gossip," in their *Moralities of Everyday Life* (New York: Oxford University Press, 1982), pp. 89–106; and Patricia Meyer Spacks, *Gossip* (Chicago: University of Chicago Press, 1985).

11   A point of which Spacks's treatment of gossip made me aware.

9. PRIVACY AND SPHERES OF LIFE

1   See Yirmiahu Yovel, *The Marrano of Reason* (Princeton: Princeton University Press, 1989), for an exploration of this issue in

the case of Jews living in inquisitorial Spain, and their descendants.

2   Beth Ann Krier, "Whose Sex Secret Is It?: Do we have a right to know a public figure's sexual orientation? Recent disclosures by gay activists, media fuel a bitter debate," *Los Angeles Times*, March 22, 1990, part E, p. 1, col. 2.

3   In the infamous *Bowers v. Hardwick* case [478 United States 1039 (1986)], the majority of the U.S. Supreme Court adopts precisely this perspective. But even the dissenters who disagree with the majority about what the ends of family privacy are see it as serving some specific end, namely, intimacy.

4   For instance, in Hegel's *Philosophy of Right* (translated by T. M. Knox [Oxford: Oxford University Press, 1952]) the right to property derives from the will's need for a domain to exercise itself upon: "45. To have power over a thing *ab extra* constitutes possession. The particular aspect of the matter, the fact that I make something my own as a result of my natural need, impulse, and caprice, is the particular interest satisfied by possession. But I as free will am an object to myself in what I possess and thereby also for the first time am an actual will, and this is the aspect which constitutes the category of *property*, the true and right factor in possession."

5   See Susan Wolf, "Asymmetrical Freedom," *Journal of Philosophy* 77 (1980), pp. 151–66.

6   This is John Austin's point about the meaning of "real." See J. L. Austin, *Sense and Sensibilia* (Oxford: Oxford University Press, 1962), pp. 70–71.

7   Berkeley Conference on Privacy, October 1990.

8   This example was suggested by a participant at the Berkeley Conference on Privacy, October 1990.

9   New York: Doubleday, 1959.

10. SPHERES OF LIFE

1   See W. T. Jones, "Public Roles, Private Roles and Differential Moral Assessments of Role Performance," *Ethics* 94 (1984), pp. 603–20.

2   See Chapter 1 for the distinction between a role and a relationship.

3   Carol Gilligan, in her book *In a Different Voice: Psychological Theory and Women's Development* (Cambridge, Mass.: Harvard

University Press, 1982), locates the difference between rule compliance and relationship maintenance as a difference between general patterns of how men and women face life. Someone might suggest that the context, not the gender, promotes these different attitudes toward interdependence and abstract rules. Alternatively, one might think the difference gender-specific and argue that our notions of public life and public rules will change as women's voices are heard in the public domains. For a comprehensive critical assessment of Gilligan's analysis, see Owen Flanagan's *Varieties of Moral Experience: Ethics and Psychological Realism* (Cambridge, Mass.: Harvard University Press, 1990), chaps. 9–11.

4 For an elegant and passionate elaboration of this standard perspective, see Stanley Benn, *A Theory of Freedom* (Cambridge: Cambridge University Press, 1988), p. 111. "The well-informed and benevolent administrator of another person's life may be able to realize states of affairs external to the agent that the latter has it as his object to bring about. But such paternalist management would be a kind of theft, stealing from their author the plans for a world in the making of which he sought the expression and realization of his own nature and identity, leaving him without a part in what he meant to be his own creation. For what the benevolent paternalist is not able to bring about, or only in a very indirect sense, is that the project be realized while yet remaining the author's own." The sort of harsh judgment of Fanny's deceit or management of Maggie that would result from the application of standards of this paragraph seems inappropriate in our context. Fanny "managed" Maggie to help Maggie be not only the author of her acts but to be a successful author of her acts.

5 Recall the insincere expression of this unboundedness in Goneril's and Regan's expression of their love to their father at the opening of the play *King Lear*. Regan declares, in part: "That I profess myself an enemy to all other joys which the most precious square of sense possesses, and find I am alone felicitate in your dear Highness' love" (Act 1, scene 1).

6 This difference is reminiscent of Carol Gilligan's characterization of differences in male and female scripts for interaction; see *In a Different Voice*.

Index

Index

Scheler, Max, 17–18, 197
Sex, pleasure in, 126–7
Sherif, Muzafer, 203
Sidgwick, Henry, 200
Silver, Maury, 99
Simmel, Georg, 108, 111, 213, 215–16
Sipple, Oliver, 154
Slote, Michael, 195
Social action, 97
Social freedom, 1–3, 114, 153
  and associative ties, 7
  conditions of, 98
Social pressure, 3, 95, 101–2
Social rationality, 100
Social tyranny, 24
Societies vs. political bodies, 96–7
Socrates, 25
Spheres of life, 155–7, 168
Steele, Claude, 86, 211–12
Stevenson, Charles, 85, 211
Stone, Lawrence, 123, 217–18

Thaler, Paul, 60
Thomas, Laurence, 42
Tribe, Laurence, 87
Trilling, Lionel, 131, 218
Tversky, Amos, 202

Ullman-Margalit, Edna, 83, 205

Value entropy, 116, 130, 134, 152
Values, personal ranking, 182
Veyne, Paul, 216

Waldron, Jeremy, 50
Watt, Ian, 131
Wertheimer, Alan, 214
Wideman, John, 92
Williams, Bernard, 85
Wollheim, Richard, 19

Zimbardo, Phillip, 58, 68
Zimmerman, Diane, 219